Basic Business Software

by
E. G. Brooner

Howard W. Sams & Co., Inc.
4300 WEST 62ND ST. INDIANAPOLIS, INDIANA 46268 USA

International Standard Book Number: 0-672-21751-1
Library of Congress Catalog Card Number: 80-52232

Printed in the United States of America.

Preface

The early 1970s saw an explosion in electronics technology with the introduction of the microprocessor integrated circuit, the so-called "computer on a chip." While at first rather expensive when compared to other integrated circuit devices, these microprocessor devices were providing undreamed of computational power in many new and exciting applications. While in 1970 a "small" computer system cost tens of thousands of dollars, today an equivalent computer system can be bought for about 1000 dollars. Microprocessor chips are being used in toys, games, appliances, and automobiles, places where the use of a computer was unheard of, if not unbelievable, just a few years ago.

Many electronics hobbyists saw the availability of microprocessor chips as a way of obtaining computer power for various projects at a small fraction of the cost of a complete computer system. Thus, in mid 1974 the "home" computer was born. Many different home computers were spawned, having names such as Jolt, KIM, IMSAI, Altair, Sphere, and others. Many small companies were quickly organized in the hopes of capitalizing on this new market for computers, memories, peripherals, and software. During the explosive growth of the home computer market, some people started to realize that the small computers that were being used by hobbyists might also be used to provide some sort of minimal computational ability to small businesses. Previously, small businesses relied upon hand (calculator) operations, or on the use of business services to provide for their computational needs.

At present, the microcomputer market has matured so that there are a number of good computer systems available at reasonable cost, and almost all of the "bugs" have been worked out of these systems so that the hardware is up and running almost as soon as the system is plugged in. Likewise, there are a number of good software packages available. These cover complex operating system programs, game programs, educational programs, and business programs aimed at the small-business person. Unfortunately, many small-business people don't know how to evaluate "off-the-shelf" business programs, and they may not be able to write any of their own software.

The purpose of this book, *Basic Business Software*, is to help business people understand some of the fundamentals of business software development. While some familiarity with BASIC-language programming is assumed, familiarity with computer technology, digital electronics, operating system software, and more complex topics are not discussed at all. The main idea is to introduce you to how business software is written so that you can either write some of your own or evaluate those programs that are available from others. Several useful programs have been provided so that the small-business person can immediately start to use a small computer system to evaluate its potential for saving time and energy. The reader may find that the programs provided are useful, but may wish to add some feature or remove another. Such adaptation and experimentation is encouraged.

While generally aimed at the business person who is interested in the use of small computers, programmers will also learn more about business software by reading this book. Careful examination of the sample programs provides a means of learning more about the design of business software. The programs stress the fact that the people using them will not be computer experts, so little can be left to the user's imagination.

Most business programs can be broken down into several general subclasses. These are information storage and retrieval, information processing, and information input and output. The uses of these three subclasses of programs are stressed throughout the book so that you can see the many similarities between a mail-list manipulation program and a general ledger program. Once the basic principles of these programs have been mastered it becomes relatively easy to specify additional functions for existing programs, and it is also fairly easy to develop your own programs.

Readers involved with small businesses will find a great deal of useful information in this book, along with the many programs that may be used by themselves. While most of the programs in this book have been written in one of the North Star BASIC dialects, they can easily be "translated" into other BASIC dialects. Several programs are provided in Microsoft BASIC. Nine business programs are provided, in complete listings, with flowcharts and documentation.

E. G. BROONER

Contents

CHAPTER 6

CHAPTER 7

CHAPTER 8

CHAPTER 9

CHAPTER 10

APPENDIX

1

Introduction to
Small-Business Software

OBJECTIVES

In this chapter, you will learn the following:

- What constitutes a small-business computer.
- What small-business software is.
- The price range of the hardware.
- The price range of the software.
- Which small businesses can benefit.

Computer programming (software) is a broad field within which programming for business applications is only a part. In its turn, business programming is divided in several ways; one such division may be called *small-business software*, for lack of a better term. Within that context there are many subheadings and directions from which to approach the subject. This text will address those persons most likely to have a common interest in business application programming, even though their background or training might not be the same. Presumably they have previously specialized in business, accounting, or general programming, but feel a bit new to the other aspects of business application programming.

Two groups make up the majority of those interested in small-business software. These are the owner/operator of a small business, and the programmer who has a need to serve such customers. Both may have a good general idea of the ways in which small computers can be used in business; that is, for accounting, inventory, and perhaps some special purposes that have occurred to them, but they have not yet grasped the means for accomplishing this. The following chapters are intended to provide some insight for both the programmer who is writing business software for the first time, and the business person or accountant who is going to use it. To do this, it is necessary to establish limits to the coverage and also to duplicate, for each reader, some of the things he or she already knows.

SMALL-BUSINESS COMPUTERS DEFINED

First of all, this discussion will be limited to what is often called the *small-business computer*. The official definition of what a small business is has to be bent a little when speaking of computers. A small business is usually described as one employing a few hundred employees and doing an annual volume of several million dollars. This definition will not do where computers are concerned. Firms fitting the description can afford, and even require, the same type of computer systems used by governments and giant corporations; however, when the computer industry talks about small business, the reference is to such entities as "mom-and-pop" stores, service stations, and operations of that size. A business of this sort may consist of the owner and either the owner's family or a very few employees. It looks like a small family operation even if it is not.

The definition really hinges on the price range of the computer that such a business can afford. In the late 1970s, this price range turned out to be the less-than-$10,000 market, although some exceptions existed. It is definitely bracketed by a price range of hundreds of dollars at one extreme, and tens of thousands of dollars at the other.

The small-business computer market grew out of the hobby movement of the 1970s. The typical hobby computer was then a "bare-bones" affair worth a few hundred dollars at most. At some point, manufacturers realized that by adding a high-level language (see Chapter 2), a printer, and a mass storage device, these erstwhile "toys" would become suitable for business use. In this manner, the small-business computer was born.

Keep in mind that it was the peripheral equipment that gave birth to the small-business computer. Although a video terminal is sufficient for hobby uses, a serious business must have "hard copy," as computer persons usually refer to anything printed on paper. And while the hobbyist could fuss with the eccentricities of cassette tape, the disk was the only medium of storage both reliable enough and cheap enough for these small businesses we have been discussing. More than anything else, the development of low-cost floppy-disk systems made the small-business market a reality. For the rest of this book, machines not having a printer and one or more disk drives will simply be ignored as not being business machines.

The buyer faces a bewildering assortment of small computers from which to choose, many at less than $1000. Of course, these are not complete business machines—adding disk drives, printers, and additional memory runs the cost up considerably. Among the leading low-cost machines is the TRS-80 marketed by Radio Shack, a division of Tandy Corp. This is probably the most popular small computer ever built, having sold a reputed 100,000 units in the first year or so of production. With the necessary accessories, the hardware cost is slightly over $3000 for a minimal, but effective, small-business computer.

A typical TRS-80 business computer system is shown in Fig. 1-1. Note that this system uses an expansion interface that is located under the video display, and two floppy-disk drives located to the right of the keyboard. The computer system would look exactly the same if it were used for scientific data processing, or some other nonbusiness task, since the business configuration is obtained simply by supplying the proper software. In this case, the business applications programs are provided in the floppy disks, available from many suppliers.

One of the earliest entries in the small-business market, and still an excellent system in the low to medium price range, is the North Star Horizon. North Star came into the market early with a reliable, five-inch floppy-disk system which soon became an industry standard. North Star was also among the first microcomputer makers to build disk drives into the computer box itself, thereby acknowledging that disks are an essential component of a small computer system. The disk system was

Courtesy Radio Shack, A Division of Tandy Corp.

Fig. 1–1. A TRS-80 microcomputer system with two floppy-disk drives.

also marketed separately and became an accessory to many thousands of computers built by other companies. By being built around the popular "S-100" bus system, both packages were assured compatibility with equipment made by dozens of other companies. The Horizon sells at less than $3000 and needs only the addition of a video terminal and printer to handle the work of most small businesses. Thus configured, the system can be purchased complete (except for software) for around $4000.

A disk-based North Star Horizon computer system, with its cover removed, is shown in Fig. 1-2. The floppy-disk drives are shown on the right side of the chassis, with the power supply shown in the rear. While the Horizon computer will accept up to 12 S-100-bus compatible computer cards, one of the slots is used for the floppy-disk controller card, which can control up to four disk drives. Additional card slots are used by the central processor card, memory cards, and cards for peripheral device control. The motherboard contains two serial input/output (I/O) ports, as well as a parallel input port and a parallel output port.

The North Star Horizon computer is shown in use in Fig. 1-3. A terminal and a printer are being used with the computer, along with the two disk drives that are a part of the computer case. As with many small computers, the Horizon does not have a complex front panel with many

Courtesy North Star Computers, Inc.

Fig. 1–2. A North Star Horizon microcomputer with cover removed.

lights and switches to confuse and confound the operator, who may have absolutely no understanding of computers. The computer system shown in Fig. 1-3 represents a typical minimum system for business use.

EFFECT ON PAPER WORK

A few other items should be clarified before getting into the subject of software. The potential computer user should not expect computerization to eliminate paper work; quite the contrary, it may increase it. One good reason for this is that anything worth keeping, in the way of records, is more useful on paper. The second reason is that computer records, no matter how carefully handled, sometimes just "go away" as the result of accidents such as power failures and operator error. The third and most compelling reason is this: paper work is tedious; most businesses would like to have more paper work except for the difficulty of its preparation, the time it consumes, and the constant possibility of errors creeping in. The computer can digest a lot of data and spit it out later in many different forms and formats. The tediousness is gone and paper work becomes a blessing rather than a curse.

BUSINESSES THAT BENEFIT

So far, we have established some limits on which businesses are concerned by the scope of this book. They are small businesses in most

Courtesy North Star Computers, Inc.

Fig. 1–3. A typical small-business computer system.

11

senses of the term. But even with the wide availability of affordable equipment, there are some other restrictions. Many small businesses will simply not benefit, at least to any large degree, from a computer. Who will? Generally speaking, the prime candidate for computerization is a business having its assets tied up in inventory, or in accounts receivable, or one that has an inordinately large customer list or mail-order clientele.

Exceptions to the size criterion are the small accounting firms, some of which have some fairly large customers. The clients of such firms, whatever their size, usually have only their ledger work and tax work done by the accountant. If he is doing only these functions and can devote the entire capability of his small computer to one large job at a time, he can handle some fairly large ones with a small machine. By the time the client wants all of his paper work computerized, he will probably have established his own data-processing section.

A largely untapped computer market is represented by the thousands of small family-size farms. There have been experimental projects by state and federal agencies in some farming areas, usually dealing with the feeding, breeding, and production of animals. Dairies are an example, as are pig- and chicken-raising operations. The accounting needed by many farms is such that it may usually be done either by hand or by computer, with little preference either way. In the future, computers on the farm will deal with those elements critical to the particular operation, and records that take into account the product mix, soil and water peculiarities, etc., which may vary from one farm to the next even if located side by side. There is room here for a great deal of creative, customized programming by either the independent programmer or by the farmer himself.

There are uncounted thousands of other small businesses that can benefit from computers—the examples in this chapter are only the "tip of the iceberg." Many opportunities are unknown to today's programmers and will not be uncovered until the proprietors themselves become computer-minded, and receive that sudden inspiration that will save time, or money, or give them a completely new control over their own rather narrow specialty. This is the excitement of small computers; their application represents an entire new frontier in the business world, one that has hardly been tapped.

SOFTWARE COSTS

One more factor must be added to the qualifications for small-business software—it must be low-cost. A price of $50,000 for software sounds reasonable for a million-dollar computer, and it is if the quality and usefulness is considered. A $5000 computer might benefit from a similar package but the scale of costs is unreasonable. Small-business software, unfortunately, has to be cheaper than the machine itself, and yet it must work well. The challenge of small-business software—to produce adequate results within the budget—will be considered again in Chapter 3.

This book, then, is for the small entrepreneur, be he a farmer, a programmer, or a businessman. Application programming may become the "cottage industry" of the future. It is a calling which can be followed at home or in the "back room," whenever time and inspiration permit. Because of numbers alone, the bulk of business programming, for the foreseeable future, will be on small machines by or for small-business people. Mass production must come eventually but will never completely replace the personal touch, any more than factories can completely eliminate skilled craftsmen.

Numerous books in this and other series explain computer logic, number systems, and specific languages. These subjects are all extremely interesting for their own sake, but the business person should not feel compelled to learn them as a prerequisite to owning a computer. In the following chapters, these subjects, although important, will be neglected in favor of putting practical programming ideas to work.

SELF-HELP TEST QUESTIONS

1. Why are low-cost computers not more widely used in business?
2. What is the price range of "small" business computers?
3. Which small businesses can benefit most from computers?
4. Must the business person be a programming "expert"?
5. Do all businesses require the same hardware and software?

2

Software Fundamentals

OBJECTIVES

This chapter deals with the software portion of the small-business computer system, what it is and how it is put together. Software is a general term covering all items that are not hardware; that is, the machine itself and its peripheral equipment, such as the printer.

SOFTWARE FUNCTIONS

Broadly defined, software is what makes the computer "do something," since the hardware is inert until it gets instructions and data. In one context, the term software means programs. Later we will discuss additional software functions which, along with programs, make up the computer's complete software system. Considering the tasks that can be performed by the small-business computer, we find that programs for the following purposes, and others, are fairly common.

1. The *accounting* functions. Regardless of the type or amount of bookkeeping to be done, a computer (properly programmed) will make the work faster, easier, and more accurate; at some very low level of business, however, it may not be worth the cost.
2. *Inventory*, particularly if inventory is a major activity. It is important to know what is on hand, what parts, products, assemblies, etc., are, what they cost, and what may be on order.

   When loan interest is high, or when additional commercial funding is not readily available, this information may spell the difference between the success or failure of a business.
3. *Payroll* is a tedious task, subject to much error because of the amount of detail and number of reports involved. Although

computerizing is no guarantee of an error-free operation, it does speed the preparation of the payroll figures and reports.

4. *File research* can be greatly enhanced by a computer data base or information file, and an appropriate means of searching or sorting the information. For example, the business of real-estate sales and management involves the *matching* of a buyer to appropriate properties.

To these uses of a business computer system must be added information storage, retrieval, and management of all kinds. Most of the examples in this book deal with the storage and retrieval of various kinds of information. Computer modeling and simulation, to be mentioned again in a later chapter, are a form of information management using hypothetical data. These activities, and others, are within the range of capabilities of all but the very smallest modern computers.

COMPUTER LANGUAGES

Whatever tasks the computer is expected to do must be described in a language that the computer can understand. At the lowest, or *machine-language* level, in which all operations are ultimately expressed, the instructions and data are all in the form of *binary numbers*. The binary numbers may have been expressed by the programmer in octal (base-8) or hexadecimal (base-16) values. The binary number, 10000001, for example, can be expressed as 201 octal, or 81 hexadecimal. Going a step further toward the human level is a system of mnemonic instructions which can be converted to binary numbers. The numbers just listed, in binary, octal, and hexadecimal, can all be represented by the mnemonic ADD. At this point, we begin to encounter systems that make a translation of sorts. In the case of mnemonic languages, the programmer can enter terms, such as ADD, into an *assembler*, a program that will translate such instructions to their numerical equivalent.

Going still further, we find the so-called "high-level" languages which permit relative ease of communication between human and machine. This is the level at which most modern programming is done.

Numbering systems and languages are covered by many books in this, and other, series and will not be discussed in detail here. Some languages are of interest as a context into which the practices of business programming can be introduced. Large computer systems, particularly in the past, used languages such as COBOL (for business programming) and FORTRAN (for scientific programming). There are many other languages, most of which are of little interest to small-business people, either because they are inappropriate or because they place unrealistic constraints on the size of the hardware.

BASIC

BASIC is the most common high-level language for small computers—it is almost the only one. The name stands for *B*eginners *A*ll-purpose *S*ymbolic *I*nstruction *C*ode, but the word *beginner* should not be misinterpreted. The language is not as simple as the name might indicate, and contrary to some misleading advertising, it cannot be learned overnight or during a long weekend. Rather than being developed for use in one particular field, such as science, BASIC was developed to be used in a variety of fields; it may not be the best choice for any particular use, but some of the advanced versions approach some of the other more specialized languages in power, particularly those versions of BASIC developed for business purposes. Business computations are usually so trivial, in computer terms, that they place no great mathematical demand on the language.

The number of different versions of BASIC can scarcely be estimated, as each maufacturer seems to provide some variations not found in other dialects. For this reason, many of the BASIC programs published in books and magazines often do not work for the reader who tries them on his own computer, even though the differences may be subtle and hard to detect.

Most of the programs in this book are in North Star BASIC, Release 4. They will work in Release 5 by North Star also, but not in Release 3 or Release 2. They will not work on any machine using any other type of BASIC without some (usually minor) changes. The fundamental statements, commands, and syntax are to a great extent the same in the various dialects of BASIC; the differences that are serious usually involve the input/output and disk-handling instructions. The best insurance of program convertability is to be thoroughly familiar with your own BASIC. Some of the more common business BASICs will be listed here; from time to time, the text will compare or refer to various dialects of BASIC that will be encountered in small-business programming.

Microsoft BASICs—This rather large family of BASICs has been developed in many versions, both for disk-based computer systems and for computers having different means of storing software. Among these varieties are BASICs provided on punched paper tape, cassette tape, or within the computer itself in ROM (*R*ead-*O*nly-*M*emory). Although these varieties are essentially the same language, the shorter versions usually omit several important commands and statements. The disk-based versions are generally quite powerful and require more memory in which to operate, largely because of the addition of disk-handling features. Most of the relatively low-priced computers on the market use some version of Microsoft BASIC, as do several systems in higher price ranges. It is probably the most frequently encountered kind of BASIC.

North Star BASICs—This family of BASICs consists of the original version, and several releases that upgrade the first version. North Star BASIC was originally conceived as a disk-based language, and the later changes are enchancements which do not preclude the use of programs written in earlier versions. North Star BASIC is found only on computers and/or disk systems marketed by North Star. Its better features are simplicity, relatively high-speed access of disk files, and relatively low price. Its manner of manipulating numbers by their BCD (Binary-Coded Decimal) representation yields more accurate mathematical results when solving some problems than do BASICs that use straight binary conversions.

C-BASIC—C-BASIC is typical of the several BASICs that have been developed especially for business use. Such dialects attempt to overcome weaknesses that might make other BASICs less than desirable for business programming. In general they require larger memories than are available on very small computers, are disk-oriented, and pay particular attention to the handling of disk files.

Other Business BASICs—There are some minicomputers, generally out of the small-business class because of size and cost, that use BASIC as a primary high-level language. Among others, DEC (Digital Equipment Corp.), IBM, Wang, and Olivetti provide fairly comprehensive BASICs which the very small business will never encounter. With all of these BASICs, the major differences are in their manner of handling string variables and disk files. Perhaps the best, and most commercially oriented BASIC, is C-BASIC. It was written for business use and differs greatly from nearly all other available dialects.

When translating from one BASIC to another, special care must be used in handling numeric data. It has been noted that the computer treats all data as binary numbers; however, there are different ways of making the conversion. Some versions of BASIC use the BCD conventions and others do not. A general rule is that the faster dialects do not use BCD and, as a result, some unexpected rounding errors are often produced. These can be disastrous when doing calculations in dollars and cents.

Although slightly slower in arithmetic functions, the BASICs using BCD arithmetic are preferred for business. Two such versions are the North Star BASIC and C-BASIC, which was developed primarily for business use.

Assembly Language

The mnemonic statements mentioned earlier help make up the family of languages known as *assembly languages*, and these mnemonic languages differ from one another by each having been written for a particular processor architecture. They are a time saver for experienced programmers but are seldom of any concern to the actual computer user. Readers interested in assembly or machine languages are referred to the books listed at the end of the chapter. These books deal with the internal working of the 8080A microprocessor, which is in widespread use as the heart of a great many small computers. Assembly language is introduced here by way of describing, in brief terms, what is known as the computer *operating system*.

THE OPERATING SYSTEM

An operating system is a machine-language program, or collection of programs, peculiar to your particular type of computer, your particular version of BASIC, and the peripherals as you have them configured. Writing an operating system is a rather advanced programming task, usually not attempted by beginning programmers, although many programmers modify such systems as a routine matter. Unless the user buys a "turnkey" system, complete with all necessary software and hardware, there will be a need to customize the system software. As an example, CP/M, one of the more standardized commercial operating systems, is delivered for use with a great many different disk systems, and a great deal of ready-made software is available for it. Nevertheless, the operating system itself must be modified slightly to work with your terminal and printer, and the ready-made programs will have to be conditioned to your particular peripherals, if there is anything unusual about them.

Unless the user simply has a desire to learn all about programming, his or her interest in the operating system may be limited to an understanding of its limitations and its compatibility with other software. BASIC, for example, is itself a machine-language program, and each version of BASIC is intended for use with a particular type of operating system.

SOFTWARE DEFINED

Following the brief discussion of languages, we are prepared for a more detailed definition of software. The term includes the fundamental machine-language or assembly-language operating system, and associated utilities. The operating system handles such chores as communicating between the program, the disk drives, the printer, and other peripherals.

Utilities are defined as the subprograms, usually a part of the operating system, which perform specific functions. The functions they perform are "housekeeping" tasks that are necessary to the system, but are not part of any high-level program. An example of a utility program is the portion of the North Star DOS (Disk Operating System) that copies the contents of one disk onto another. It is invoked by simply typing CD (for *Copy Disk*) and the number of the source drive and the number of the destination drive.

Another common utility on many computer systems is a memory test. Some systems have been written in such a manner that a utility subprogram (such as a file-sorting routine) can be accessed on demand by the main program, or programs.

The high-level language (such as BASIC) and the programs themselves are also described as software. Included, too, are the operator instructions whether they are bound in a book, printed on the screen during program operation, or in the form of remarks and comments listed within the program itself. The somewhat ambiguous term, *firmware*, usually refers to more-or-less permanent and unchangeable software.

Documentation is an important aspect of any software. Although the original programmer may have understood what he meant and how the program was to be used, the same may not apply to subsequent users. One of the most common complaints, as far as business users are concerned, is that the operator instructions are inadequate. A program that is obscure in its actions, or that is difficult to implement, will not gain any fervent supporters of computer science and probably will not result in the benefits the business had a right to expect.

LANGUAGE-INDEPENDENT PROGRAMMING

The computer user (or potential user) who has no training in programming should not be intimidated by its mysteries. The best way to learn is to take a course from a nearby college, if one is available. Such courses may also be available at a local computer club or at a computer store. Among the reference books listed at the end of the chapter, the reader will find texts which deal with learning BASIC in an informal manner. If time and circumstance do not permit the study of a high-level language, the end user is still not completely out of the picture. The very best programmers usually start by carefully defining the problem in their native language.

The problem should be stated as precisely as possible. In the case of a payroll, for example, the statement, "Calculate the pay for each employee," leaves a lot to the imagination. A better expression would be, "Identify the employee and his hourly rate, input the hours worked, multiply by hourly rate to find gross pay," and so on, through the standard deductions, the state tax, federal tax, etc.

When the problem has been defined, a detailed outline can be drawn up, still in your native language. Not until this is done should any actual program code be written. At this point, even if you, as the end user, must turn the job over to a programmer, the job has been greatly simplified and a better program is assured.

BASIC COMPARISON AND TRANSLATION

Most of the example programs in this book are in North Star BASIC, Release 4. Each time North Star upgrades their BASIC, they manage to keep all the previous features intact; hence, Release 3 programs will work in Release 4 and in Release 5, but Release 5 programs may not work in earlier versions. North Star BASIC is believed by many to be one of the better BASICs for business programming, and this upward compatibility may well account for some of its popularity.

BASICs by Microsoft are widely used, particularly in popular, low-cost systems. They are not necessarily compatible with one another, but the differences are slight. They do differ as a group from North Star and from other completely independent systems. Two common computers using derivations of Microsoft BASIC are the Radio Shack computers and the Commodore Pet-2001. This family of BASICs also appears in conjunction with some other more-or-less standard operating systems, such as CP/M.

BASICs can be broadly categorized in two classes—*interpreters* and *compilers*. Compiler languages are slightly more sophisticated and, some believe, more professional. Their distinguishing feature is that before the program can be run, the original program (called the *source*) has to be *compiled* (by system software). This consists of translating it into a machine-language form as a body. The result is yet another program, called the *object code*, which is usually shorter and runs faster than the source and is unreadable in human terms. Program modifications require a complete recompilation of the source code.

One of the best known compiler BASICs is C-BASIC, by Lifeboat Associates. High-quality small-business software is frequently written in C-BASIC.

Interpreters, on the other hand, translate BASIC programs into machine-language code as the program runs. This makes errors easier to detect and correct, as the program simply stops when an error is detected. Interpreter languages are usually simpler to implement and owe their popularity to this feature.

Major Variations

The most serious variations between different BASICs involve *file-handling* and *string-handling* conventions. Translating between different BASICs requires some understanding of the original language and the one into which the program is to be translated. For example:

String Arrays—Most, if not all, of the Microsoft BASICs permit string arrays; that is, lists of the contents of several string variables, stored in an array. Each string can be of any length, up to 256 bytes. Neither the string nor the number of strings need be defined in advance. However, the space for their storage must be reserved. The statement for this is

CLEAR XX, where XX is the amount of space to reserve.

North Star requires that strings over 10 bytes long be dimensioned as follows: DIM A$(15). This reserves a 15-byte space for A$. The string, A$, can be of any length that will fit into memory, as long as the desired length is stated in advance. String arrays as such are not supported, but can be simulated, for example, by dimensioning a string as 100 bytes in length, and then using the first 10 bytes as substring 1, the second 10 bytes as substring 2, etc.

Microsoft BASICs describe portions of a string as follows: LEFT$(A$,10) is the leftmost 10 characters in A$. Similar statements describe the rightmost and middle characters. In North Star BASIC, the same portion of A$ is A$(1,10). The last 10 bytes (or substring 10 in a 100-byte string) are described as A$(91,100).

File Statements—Example 2-1 will demonstrate the differences between these two systems, assuming that we wish to store the following variables in a random-access file. The variables are A, B, and C (numeric) and A$, B$, and C$, (string variables) of less than 10 bytes each in length. This example assumes that the record is the first record in the data file and that this file's records are to be 60 or less bytes in length.

Example 2-1. Typical File Statements
(A) North Star

```
A$ = (string)\B$ = (string)\C$ = (string)
WRITE#1%60,A,B,C,A$,B$,C$
```

(B) Microsoft

```
FIELD#1, 4 AS A1$, 4 AS B1$, 4 AS C1$,
   10 AS A$, 10 AS B$, 10 AS C$
LSET A1$ = MKS$(A):LSET B1$ = MKS$(B):LSET
   C1$ = MKS$(C)
LSET A$ = (string):LSET B$ = (string):LSET
   C$ = (string)
PUT #1,1
```

The Microsoft disk BASIC used by the Radio Shack TRS-80 Model I computer is identical with the Microsoft example just discussed, except that the statements are FIELD 1, and PUT 1, without the pound signs (#). This family of BASICs uses slightly less file space than would be the case for the same variables in North Star, but the program is somewhat more complex.

Another common difference is that encountered when formatting PRINT statements. We wish to print a variable, N, whose value is 97.61 at its first occurrence, and 86.00 on its second occurrence. Example 2-2 illustrates how the numbers are formatted by two different BASICs.

Example 2-2. Typical Print Formatting Statements
(A) Microsoft

PRINT USING "###.##"; N

(B) North Star

PRINT %7F2,N

Both of these statements would print N as follows:

97.61
86.00

Of course, any BASIC can print N with the statement, PRINT N; the formats shown in Example 2-2 provide for two decimal places even if zeros are to appear after the decimal point. This results in a better appearance when dollar and cents quantities are being printed. The statement, "PRINT N," without formatting, would result in the following:

97.61
86

A fourth major difference in BASICs involves *line numbering*. BASIC statements are usually numbered sequentially, such as 10, 20, 30, etc. If it is desired to insert a line between 10 and 20 later, it can be called 15 and the program puts it in correct order. But, what if we want 11 lines, or program statements, between statements 10 and 20? A great many BASICs permit a "renumber" command which rearranges the spacing. In North Star, this statement is REN. In some Microsoft BASICs, it is RENUM. Some do not support this feature.

C-BASIC, mentioned earlier, does not require line numbers at all unless the statement is to be referred to, as in GOTO 100. Those that need to be referenced can be numbered as 100, 200, etc. If space becomes cramped, this BASIC even permits fractional line numbers, as in 100.1, 100.2, and so forth.

Internal Arithmetic—A fifth and not so apparent difference in BASICs involves the *internal arithmetic*. Although not immediately evident, it has a lot of bearing on how a language performs. All computers deal with binary numbers internally, but converting from decimal values (preferred by humans) can be done in different ways.

The result may be as illustrated here. A number, 1.01, is to represent a date, January 1. To edit this for the month and the day, we wish to take the integer of the number (1) and subtract it from the original figure, leaving, we hope, .01 as the remainder. If this is done using BCD representation, all will be well. We can then multiply the .01 by 100 and end up with a 1 for the day. But, if BCD representation is not used, the problem may result in 1 for the month, and 9.99999E − 03 to represent the .01 value. Multiplying this by 100 will obviously result in .999999 or some similar amount. We can avoid this (if we have to) by adding .1 to the remainder to yield some number such as 1.00009 and then taking the integer of that number as the day. There are also other ways of making the conversion. If no calculations are to use the number, it can be forced to be printed as a 1 by using the print image, ##.##. In general, these more "tricky" BASICs operate faster, but the program itself is a little complex to write.

Minor Differences

Variable Names—In all BASICs, variables are of two types—numeric and string. A numeric variable might be called A. In nearly all BASICs, there can also be A1, A2, A3, and so on. Some families of BASIC permit, in addition, variables such as AA, AB, and AC, and these combinations allow many more variables to be designated. Microsoft BASICs usually permit this kind of variable to be used. Translations into another dialect may require the use of different variable names. In some cases, up to five letters may be used to make up a variable name. (ABCDE might have meaning to the programmer, although the program recognizes only the first two characters as being unique.) Care must be used to avoid such variable names as TOTAL or FORMS, as their leading characters might be interpreted by some BASICs as representing TO or FOR statements. Such a misunderstanding would result in a syntax error message.

Following a letter with a dollar sign, of course, means in most (if not all) BASICs that the variable is a string quantity.

C-BASIC and perhaps some others permit long variable names, both for numeric and string quantities. In C-BASIC the variable representing total gross pay, in a payroll program, can be called "TOTAL.GROSS. PAY" and the name-and-address field can be described as "NAME.AND.ADDRESS$". The value of long variable names is obvious, particularly for use in programs having a great many variables.

Another minor variation is the use of the RESTORE statement. In some dialects, this restores the data pointer to the beginning of the first data statement. In others, RESTORE 400 will start reading data at line 400, even though there may be several previous data lines.

Unless a feature has been completely omitted, most of the remaining differences are self-evident. To print on the printer, rather than on the screen, the PRINT instruction may be used as PRINT #1 (North Star), LPRINT (Microsoft BASICs), or LPRINTER (C-BASIC). PRINT is used sometimes as a means of writing in a file; such use is usually obvious, and should not be confused with ordinary printing.

Some of these differences can be seen by comparing the programs listed in this book. While the differences listed here are by no means all that will be encountered when using a number of different dialects of

BASIC, they are typical of the differences encountered on small machines. The user's best assurance of successful translation is to be thoroughly familiar with his own version of BASIC; differences will then immediately be apparent whenever a translation is made.

The following chapters will deal both with writing business software and buying or modifying ready-made programs, sometimes referred to as *canned programs*. The business person wishing to learn programming will find it a rewarding experience that, nevertheless, demands time and effort. The programmer just getting into business software may also find the learning experience worthwhile. Both operating a business and programming a computer are exact and logical sciences which go well together.

SELF-HELP TEST QUESTIONS

1. What sort of "language" is used internally by computers?

2. What is an operating system?

3. What is a high-level language?

4. Why do programs for one machine sometimes fail to work on a different one?

5. Name some small-business functions for which a computer is especially useful.

REFERENCES

1. Coan, J.S. *Basic BASIC*, 2nd ed. Hayden Book Co., Inc., Rochelle Park, NJ, 1978.

2. Kemeny, J. G.; Kurtz, T.E. *BASIC Programming*, 2nd ed. John Wiley & Sons, Inc., New York, 1971.

3. Leventhal, L. A. *8080A/8085 Assembly Language Programming*. Osborne/McGraw-Hill, Inc., Berkely, CA.

4. Rony, P. R. *The 8080A BUGBOOK®: Microcomputer Interfacing and Programming*. Howard W. Sams & Co., Inc., Indianapolis, 1977.

3

How to Choose Appropriate
Business Software

OBJECTIVES

This chapter explains the following:

- Where and how to obtain business software.
- When custom programming is necessary.
- How to tell if a program is compatible with your machine.
- What software costs, and why.

It costs more to program a computer than it does to build one. Computer prices have dropped steadily for at least two decades, and after each technical advance the new technology has been rapidly and cheaply mass-produced. No one has yet discovered an equally efficient way to produce software. Software is still hand labor; hand labor is expensive and is even more so when it involves the training and skill of a programmer. The hard truth of the matter is that programming simply cannot be done rapidly and still be done well, and does not lend itself easily to mass production.

PRACTICAL LIMITS

By some unspoken and unwritten rule, a single *application package* for a small computer has to cost considerably less than the machine. By adding several other packages—say inventory, word processing, accounting, and so on—the total software cost can easily equal or exceed the hardware cost.

Let us suppose that the world's best programmers got together, pooled their resources, and wrote a general ledger program that covered all possible eccentricities of every business. The program would be so large that only the largest machines could run it, and even then each customer would want some special amendments. In actual fact, that closely describes the history of early business software on the larger machines, and is one reason it was so expensive.

On the other hand, individual customers could have programs custom written for their particular business and exact hardware configuration, to include exactly the system that they and their bookkeeping staff had evolved, but it would cost more than it was worth. As a general rule, both approaches are so impractical as to be ruled out at the very beginning, at least for a small business.

Real life is always a compromise, and if there is any single answer to the software paradox, it is to mix custom features with standard ones that already exist. Business software, and in particular small-business software, relies on a mixture of production and marketing techniques that are still in the process of being refined.

WHERE TO GET IT

Software can generally be purchased in computer stores or from mail-order firms, or it can be written by consultants or by the owner or employees of the business. Unless the buyer or user is simply curious, nothing should ever be purchased that has either not been seen in operation, or that has already earned a good reputation. As a general rule, the selling price is a good indication of quality, but there are some horrendous exceptions at each extreme. Perhaps the best all-around approach for the business person is to purchase hardware and off-the-shelf software from the same vendor, and to have it slightly modified to suit his or her exact purpose. The business person may also have to make some slight changes in his or her paperwork (usually an improvement) to accommodate the particular computer that is to be used.

This does not necessarily imply that custom software has no place in the scheme of things. To the contrary, it is the only way some objectives can be met. At the time of this writing there is available an absolutely outstanding payroll package selling for only a few hundred dollars—a "best buy" by almost any standard. However, it places constraints on the hardware and operating system that only the better machines can meet.

There is available another even better buy, a $50.00 payroll software package that is much less elaborate and much more limited in its capability. Both payroll systems follow the common tradition (see Chapter 7) of calculating hourly wages and figuring deductions by tax tables. Neither set of programs can meet the requirement of the businesses that pay wages in some other way; that is, by percentage, by ton/mile, or by any of the other unusual ways some businesses operate.

Those businesses, if they computerize, need a custom program. We might add that errors, omissions, and "bugs" have been found in both of the payroll programs mentioned here, with considerably more "bugs" being encountered in the smaller one.

WHEN CUSTOMIZING IS NEEDED

In a situation that does not follow standard accounting, paying, or other paperwork procedures, custom software is the only way to go, although it may not be worth the full labor put into it. After it has been created, the owner of the program can try to recover the development cost by selling copies to similar businesses, and may eventually profit before running out of "similar" businesses.

On the other hand, there are a great many very ingenious business people who have a unique idea for computerization that simply has not occurred to the average programmer. This calls for custom work, if it is to be done at all. The customer and programmer who collaborate on some of these very specialized (and frequently profitable) uses may possibly uncover a previously hidden market that will make them very wealthy.

These words are not intended to discourage anyone or to hold out any false hopes. The market for software is insatiable and probably always will be. There are many sources and there will always be room for improvement and expansion. Application programs are needed for every facet of business; the best way to get started is to inspect all that is available to you, and to try writing some. As your skill improves, each effort will be better than the last one, and soon you will be able to either buy, modify, or write from scratch, software for almost any application that may present itself.

One very serious flaw in some of the best software available is a failure to consider the operator. Whether buying a program or writing one, always keep in mind the persons who will be using it. Their jobs should (hopefully) be made simpler, not more complex, and how they feel about the program and how it works for them has a lot to do with its success or failure.

There should be a foolproof set of instructions, but these instructions should not have to be used all the time. The running program should provide enough detail, in the form of prompts (messages to the operator), to permit a reasonably careful person to find his or her way through it.

In most cases, the operator will not be familiar with programming. Something used only periodically (such as a payroll) should be plain and simple enough to use that the manual need not be consulted each time the program is run. Always consider those who will be using the program, as well as their interest and level of skill.

COMPATIBILITY

Reference has been made to the incompatibility of some programs with some hardware. Purchased software should be checked for the following:

1. *Printer Width*—Your printer may accommodate 80 or fewer columns on a page, while the program may require a 120- or 132-column format.
2. *Screen Size and Configuration*—Video terminals are commonly 16 lines by 64 columns, or 24 by 80. Programs for one size may not work well on the other.
3. *Cursor control*—Some software contains cursor commands which enable some "fancy" crt displays. Your terminal must be capable of responding to such instructions, if programs require it.
4. *Disk Size and Number*—Even some fairly simple disk-based programs require more than one disk, with the program being on one and the data files on another. Programs on 8-inch disks often cannot be converted to the smaller 5-inch size.
5. *Memory Size*—Some software requires more memory than may be available in the machine it is to be used with.

These hardware considerations are in addition to making sure the software is in the proper dialect of BASIC and runs with the *operating system* you have. (The operating system communicates between the program software and various elements of the computer hardware.) Modifications are always possible, but why incur additional effort and cost when it can be avoided?

Finally, how much should business software cost? While this book was being prepared, most usable packages were in the range of hundreds of dollars, with really good custom software costing several times that figure. Attempts are being made to mass-distribute similar material in the range of $25.00 to $100. In most instances, such material has been quite general in scope and has required at least some customizing, at a cost usually at least equal to the original price. Earlier cautions still apply; if possible, buy a software package only after seeing it work.

Another worthwhile precaution is to be skeptical of claims that the package is "easily customized," unless your purchase is conditional on a fixed price for the customizing and a guarantee that it will work. Less caution is needed if you know that your own programming experience is adequate for the task.

In the following chapters, programming practices will be considered in detail for those wishing to have more control over their programs. The level of explanation will be based on the assumption that the reader has at least some familiarity with the programming language, BASIC, or has some readily available programming assistance.

SELF-HELP TEST QUESTIONS

1. Why is software relatively expensive?
2. When is custom programming necessary?
3. Name three sources of business software.
4. Why is not all software compatible with all hardware?
5. What should the business person have to spend for programs?

4

How Programs Are Put Together

OBJECTIVES

This chapter will describe the following:

- Commonly used system symbols.
- Commonly used flowchart symbols.
- The step-by-step approach to writing a program.
- Some useful programming and debugging techniques.
- The disk subsystem.

After covering this material we will go on in Chapter 5 with the application of these principles to practical business problems.

TERMS DEFINED

- *I/O (input/output)* refers to the process of getting information into the computer, from any source, and out again to the screen, printer, or other external device.
- *Subroutines* are segments of a program which stand alone in performing functions within a program that may be repeated several times.
- *Debugging* is the general process of finding and correcting "bugs," or errors, that may occur in writing or using a program.
- *Error traps* are one means of detecting programming errors and, hopefully, preventing them from disrupting the proper execution of the program.
- *Structure* and *modularity* are terms sometimes used in discussing programming. They simply mean that the program is organized in a

logical manner, and that as far as is possible, each function is clearly separated from other functions.

Within the context of the terms just defined, good subroutines may be considered to be modules, and their arrangement, along with the rest of the program, may constitute the program structure. In larger systems the term may acquire different meanings.

THE USE OF SYMBOLS IN PROGRAMMING

Programmers use a number of symbols to express in a simple and standard manner the purpose and design of a program. A distinction is made between those symbols describing an overall system, and those that show exactly how a program works. Fig. 4-1 shows the more common system symbols, while Fig. 4-2 illustrates the use of these symbols in a system diagram of the program, "CHECKING," which will be described in more detail later.

Keyboard

The keyboard is part of nearly all business computers, of whatever size. Although larger installations may input signals from paper tape, punched cards, and external equipment, the small computer is almost invariably controlled from a keyboard. It is the principal means of entering data, and may be the only such means in the system.

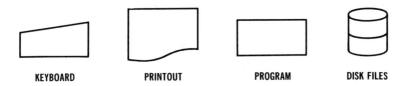

Fig. 4–1. Common system symbols.

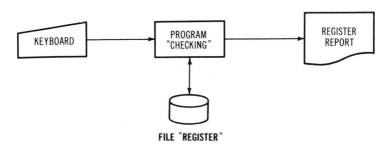

Fig. 4–2. System diagram of the program, "CHECKING."

Disk System and Disk File

The use and application of a small-business computer will nearly always depend on one or more disk drives for mass data storage. The disk *subsystem*, described more fully later in this chapter, includes the actual disks, the disk drive or drives, and the hardware needed to interface the subsystem to the remainder of the overall computer system.

Printed Output

The symbol for a printed report can also mean information printed on the video screen. In all cases, the report symbol will indicate output of some importance, and usually of some permanence, in contrast to the brief messages to the operator that may appear on the screen from time to time.

With a combination of these symbols, the program designer describes the major components of the system, as configured for this particular purpose. Notice that these symbols can represent hardware configurations as well as the major program functions. The system charts for several different applications may look very much alike, but they are nevertheless useful as a quick description of the application.

Common *flowchart* symbols are shown in Fig. 4-3. These symbols are used to explain, in a brief way, how the program actually works. If explanatory notes are added, a flowchart of this kind can describe a program in considerable detail.

I/O Symbol (Parallelogram)

This symbol always represents some sort of input or output. It can refer to reading from, or writing to, a disk or tape, printing on the printer or screen, or any similar operation. When there is doubt as to the function, flowchart notes or the program code itself can be used to narrow the definition.

Program Function Symbol

The rectangle indicates that some definite function is taking place;

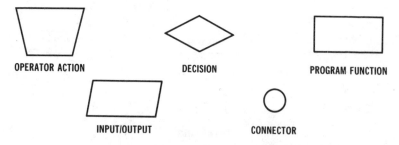

OPERATOR ACTION   DECISION   PROGRAM FUNCTION

INPUT/OUTPUT   CONNECTOR

Fig. 4–3. Common flowchart symbols.

usually, but not always, it is a mathematical function. It may define one of the structural blocks of the program. As before, explanatory notes may accompany its use.

Decision Symbol

The diamond-shaped symbol tells us that the program, at the point indicated in the flowchart, will make a decision. It does this by evaluating the result of a calculation or data that has been input by the operator.

THE STEP-BY-STEP METHOD

Designing a program is a logical step-by-step process. Programmers may be tempted to simply place themselves at the console and write code as it occurs to them. This may suffice for simple familiar uses, but it will invariably lead to trouble when dealing with a new or complex problem. The necessary steps are described in the order in which they should occur in the following paragraphs. Following this procedure will impose a certain amount of discipline which will pay off in superior results.

Defining the Problem

The problem must be clearly defined. The example program to be developed in this chapter, and in Chapter 5, can be initially described as follows:

The program will deal with a sum of money and transactions involving the money. The objective is to account for the money under the general term of *checking account*. The money in the account will be called the *balance*. The record of transactions will be known as a *check register*. From time to time, checks will be written, which will reduce the balance. At other times, additional money will be placed in the account; the term *deposit* describes this action, which increases the balance.

The checks will be dated and numbered sequentially, and they will indicate the amount of money involved and the activity for which the check was drawn. Deposits will also be dated, but will not be numbered. On occasion, a third type of activity will be involved; the bank will deduct *charges* which are neither checks nor deposits. At any time, the check register, which is maintained on a disk file within the computer, may be printed showing the previous transactions and the current balance.

The Outline

At this point in program development it is necessary to write a brief outline in one's native language; the previous paragraph having been rearranged to serve this purpose, as follows:

1. The check register will record all checking account transactions; that is, checks, deposits, and bank charges.
2. Before making any transaction, the program will open the register and read the most recent entry and the new balance (funds in the account).
3. After each transaction, the amount (if a check) will be entered into the register with date, description, amount, and the sequential check number.
4. If the transaction is a deposit, it will contain the same data as for a check, except that deposits will not be numbered.
5. When notified of bank charges, they will be entered into the register showing the date, description, and amount. Checks and bank charges will be subtracted from the balance (money in the account), and deposits will be added to the previous balance. A strategy for treating bank charges as unnumbered checks will be provided.
6. Let B1 be the previous balance, let C represent the amount of the check, and let D be the deposit.
7. Provide a means of identifying each transaction and using it with B1 to determine the new balance, B.
8. Provide a means of reading and/or printing the check register. Each such listing should show the most recent transactions and the new balance.

SUBROUTINES, OR MODULES

Although the checking program is to be developed in the next chapter, we can at this time identify the modules it will require. Some of the modules will be subroutines. We will identify these functions from the outline just prepared. The program must be able to:

1. Choose to read from, or write into, the check register.
2. Read the last entry from the file.
3. Print or display the last entry.
4. Input the data for the next entry.
5. Write the new data into the file.
6. Read and display the entire file or any part of it.

These functions are not necessarily in the order they will appear in the program. In actual practice, the operator will have some control over the order in which functions are to be performed.

Of course, there is more to it than is shown here. If someone were to be handed a checkbook for the first time, each step would have to be elaborated at some length. So it is with the program—no detail can be left to the imagination.

PROGRAMMING HINTS

Use of Remarks

It is assumed at this point that the reader has at least some acquaintance with BASIC or a similar programming language and is familiar with the fundamentals of programming. A textbook explaining BASIC statements will be helpful in understanding the following section if a reference is needed.

To make the program logical and understandable, actual program lines should be liberally interspersed with remarks, abbreviated REM in most BASICs. Remarks are used as in Example 4-1. Note that if we add the statement, 1040 RETURN, lines 1000 through 1040 become a subroutine which can be accessed from any part of the program. The practical value is that the subroutine can be repeated whenever some blank lines are desired.

Example 4-1. Using Remarks to Identify Modules

```
1000 REM PRINT 4 BLANK LINES
1010 FOR X = 1 TO 4
1020 PRINT
1030 NEXT X
```

Example 4-2 is a portion of the "NAMELIST" program described and listed later in the book. Remarks explain what the activity will be and introduce the portion of the program that deals with sorting the names into alphabetical order.

Example 4-2. Using Remarks as Program Notes

```
1470 REM SORT ROUTINE BEGINS HERE
1480 REM START BY SETTING ARRAYS
1490 REM CONVERT FIRST LETTER TO ASCII VALUE
1500 REM FOR NUMERIC SORT
```

Error Traps

We have discussed the necessity of plain-language documentation to prevent confusing the operator, and one more such warning is necessary. You, as the programmer, probably understand your program very well, but a stranger may not. If the program calls for input from the keyboard, it should "prompt" the operator with a message on the screen, telling just what is wanted. Believe it or not, some programs ask for input with no clue, on the screen or in the documentation, as to the nature of the data. Besides indicating the type of data and its limits (that is, a number, 0 to 999), "traps" should be written into the code so as to reject erroneous inputs. Example 4-3 is typical of this technique.

Example 4-3. An Example of an Operator Input Trap

```
100 PRINT "INPUT UNIT VALUE, 0 TO 999"
110 INPUT N
120 IF N>999 or N<0 THEN 100
```

These three program lines ask the operator to input a number, N, and state that it must be between 0 and 999. If it is a negative number, or a number greater than 999, the question will be repeated, and the operator will not be permitted to go past this point in the program until an acceptable number has been entered. (If the number must be an integer, add IF N<>INT (N) THEN 100.)

Another practical example asks for the date to be input as in the following paragraphs. The "traps" in this case are written so that the month has to be in the range of 1 to 12, and the day between 1 and 31. This will not prevent the operator from entering a wrong date, but it will preclude an *impossible* date.

For example, the program may ask for the current date to be input. It might be like this: DATE ?

What should the reply be, Nov 30th, 11/30/80, or something else? The following statement is much more acceptable: ENTER DATE AS MM.DD.

The program shown in Example 4-4 tells the operator to input the date as a decimal number. This technique of entering a date permits the month to be separated for sorting or for some other purpose. The important feature, however, is that the operator knows just what kind of input is expected.

Example 4-4. Date Input Program Steps

```
50 PRINT "ENTER DATE (MM.DD)"
60 INPUT D
70 M = INT (D)
80 N = 100* (D-M)
90 IF M<1 OR M>12 THEN 50
100 IF N<1 OR N>31 THEN 50
110 REM N IS NOW THE DAY AND M THE MONTH
```

In Example 4-4, D is converted to M for the month and to N for the day. No month other than 1 to 12 is permitted, and no day other than 1 to 31 is permitted. If an impossible date is entered, the operator is simply prompted to make a new entry. Alternatively, the program may print a message, such as "MONTH OUT OF RANGE" or "DATE OUT OF RANGE."

Another common method of entering a date is to ask for the month and the day as two separate quantities. It should be noted that the date is crucial to many business activities. Once the date has been entered, on any given business day, the programs can be made to automatically insert the correct date into data records and/or printed reports.

Most versions of BASIC will reject string data if a number is expected, but the reverse is never true. It is a simple matter to trap erroneous numbers. If, as in Example 4-3, 0 to 999 is desired, a single program line will reject any number out of bounds and will reprompt the operator. Program space used for this purpose is well spent. Another strategy used by some programmers is to input everything as a string, and convert it later to its numerical value, if it is indeed supposed to be a number.

A string can be "trapped" by length. Using the statement, IF LEN (A$)>10 THEN . . . (line number), will transfer control to the designated line if A$ is more than 10 characters long.

Most versions of BASIC provide some means of converting between numbers and strings. Example 4-5 illustrates this feature.

Example 4-5. String-to-Value Conversion Steps

2000 LET X$ = "123"

This statement converts the number, 123, to a string (character) value, which is desirable for certain kinds of printing. In string form, the number is easily combined with text. If X$ is the day of the month and M$ = "June," the date can be printed as PRINT M$ + X$.

The statement, 1010 LET X=VAL (X$), converts the string representation of "123" back to a number for mathematical use, if the string is indeed a number.

The statement, X$ = STR$ (123), converts the number 123 back to the string, "123," that is, *typed characters* rather than a numeric value that can be used internally by the computer. Notice that this statement serves a purpose similar to that of line 2000 in Example 4-5 but does so in a slightly different manner.

Example 4-6 is another useful conversion for turning a letter into a number. The *ASCII code* is the numeric representation for each *keyboard character;* in ASCII, each letter, number, and symbol has a numeric equivalent. Since the ASCII value for B is larger than the value for A, and the value for C in turn is larger than that for B, the ASCII values will be used to sort names in the program, "NAMELIST," which will be presented in Chapter 5.

Example 4-6. Obtaining the ASCII Value for a Letter

2020 LET A$ = "A"
2030 LET X = ASC (A$)

The variable, X, now has a numerical value equal to the value of the letter A in the ASCII table.

SUMMARY OF THE STEP-BY-STEP METHOD

Let us briefly review what has been described as a step-by-step process for writing programs. First, define the problem that the program is to handle. The definition must be exact, not approximate.

Second, outline the program in plain language, describing each step exactly, and in the proper order, if order is important. This is the proper time to determine the limits of numbers that will be permitted, as we did in the traps, Examples 4-3 to 4-4. It is not necessary to do so in the form of program lines until later. A sentence such as "limit date to 12 months and 31 days" will remind the programmer of the need for an error trap.

Third, complete a system diagram and a flowchart. Not until all of these steps are completed should any attempt be made to write code. If any printing is required, this is also the time to lay out the desired format on a piece of paper so that the correct spacing may be called for when that part of the code is written. Forms known as *print planning charts* are available for this purpose; ordinary graph paper will do as well.

Having developed the concept this far, the programmer is ready to write the program. He or she has decided, by now, the purpose of the program, what data is to be input, and in what form; the names of the key variables are known (B1, B, C, and D in the checking program), and the format of the printed report(s) is determined. Let us temporarily assume that the program has been written, as it will be in Chapter 5, and proceed to make it work.

DEBUGGING HINTS AND OTHER TECHNIQUES

It is axiomatic in programming that programs do not usually work the first time they are tried. This leads to "debugging," or finding and fixing the errors. If careful inspection fails to reveal the flaw, or flaws, it is necessary to build some temporary "bug traps" into the program.

A good place to start is with the subroutines, which have hopefully been grouped conveniently and identified with remarks. Temporary lines can be inserted at the beginning and end of each; they can be simple, just printing the line number at which they reside. They may be simple STOP statements. Most BASICs permit some sort of CONTINUE statement after a STOP. While the program is stopped, your BASIC will probably permit printing the value of a variable with a direct PRINT command. This sort of technique will at least trace the program flow and determine if it is getting to every place it should. Thus, if it gets "lost" between any two logical segments, the task of locating the error has been greatly reduced. It is also useful to print the value of certain variables, or the results of calculations, at points where they occur in the program.

Assume that a program loop is to be executed 10 times and a calculation performed for each iteration of the loop. Causing the loop index (from 1 to 10) to be printed, along with the result of the calculation, might reveal that the program is failing on a particular iteration of the loop. Many versions of BASIC contain a TRACE or ONERR (on error) feature as an aid to troubleshooting programs. These differ so widely that each is a separate case; they can be a help.

Every programmer has his or her favorite debugging tricks which have been learned by hard experience. Following the programming hints in this chapter will not eliminate bugs, but it will make them easier to find. If any one technique can be considered superior or universal, it is the liberal use of remarks.

THE DISK SUBSYSTEM

Disk systems have such an impact on software that they may be included in software discussions even though, technically, they are hardware. Disk storage has supplanted tape in small installations because it is faster, more reliable, and easier to use than cassette tape, and less expensive than high-quality tape systems.

The business system will have application programs stored on disk, and will use the same disk, or additional disks, for data storage and retrieval. It should be obvious that programs or data files made on one machine can be readily transferred to another, but only if each of the parameters—size, speed, operating system, and so on—are identical in both systems.

As a general description, the disk is round, thin, and magnetically coated on one or both sides, and data is written in concentric circular tracks. Although there is a physical resemblance to phonograph records, the read/write technique is analogous to tape-recording methods.

There are many kinds of disk systems in use. One logical classification is the distinction between "hard disks" and "soft disks." Within each of these major types, there is a further distinction based on size and another based on the format.

- *Hard Disk*—A rigid, magnetically coated surface that rotates at a very high speed, within a sealed enclosure.
- *Soft*, or *Flexible Disk*—A cheaper and more portable version of the hard disk. Soft disks usually have lower speed and less dense data storage than the hard variety. They are presently much less expensive, a distinction which may soon disappear.
- *Format* (of disks)—A definition of the way in which the surface is subdivided for the purpose of data storage.
- *Sector*—The divisions that are made when a disk is formatted.
- *Hard-Sectored*—Paradoxically, this term applies to soft disks. It

means that there is an actual physical separation between sectors, usually in the form of a machine-readable hole.

- *Soft-Sectored*—The sectors are defined by marks written on the surface by the operating system.
- *Diskettes; Floppy Disks*—Jargon used to describe soft disks.

In addition to the differences just noted, there are various ways of encoding and writing data on disks, different spacing between written tracks, different data densities, and different rotational speeds. When these variables are combined with the differences in operating systems, mentioned earlier, it can be seen that software written for any one combination of disk features may well be incompatible with any other combination of features. If both computer systems are similar enough, in both hardware and operating software, it may be possible to transfer disks and/or programs from one system to the other.

As a general rule, small-business computer systems will have disk storage in some size and form; although there have been experiments with other sizes (some as small as 3 inches), 5-inch and 8-inch diameter diskettes are the most commonly encountered. They will be of the "floppy" variety; soft plastic in a protective envelope, magnetically coated, and fairly inexpensive to buy and use.

The previously more expensive hard disks are becoming available in the small-business hardware price range, and may eventually replace soft disks for many purposes. In turn, disks of whatever kind may be made obsolete by "bubble" memory or some as yet unheard of technique.

Fig. 4-4 is a representation of part of a typical disk; it shows both hard and soft sectoring (which in practice will not be on the same disk) and the arrangement of recording tracks.

The use and handling of disk media will be described in Chapter 5.

SELF-HELP TEST QUESTIONS

1. Programs need not be logical. True or false?
2. Disk memory can be removed from the computer and used in another similar machine. True or false?
3. What part of the software system communicates directly with the disks?
4. What advantage, if any, do disks have over tape storage?
5. What should be the first step in generating a new program?

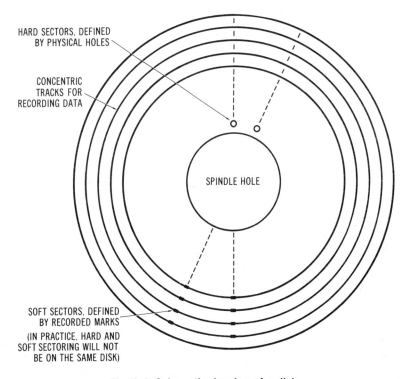

Fig. 4–4. Schematic drawing of a disk.

5

Information Storage
and Retrieval

OBJECTIVES

Upon completion of Chapter 5, the reader should understand the following:

- How information is stored.
- How it is retrieved for later use.
- How to store and handle diskettes.
- How to design the structure of a disk file.
- The fundamentals of sorting data.

Information storage and retrieval are fundamental to business software. In the past, we have thought of computers in terms of massive mathematical tasks. Writers of early books and articles were fond of describing a particular computer in terms of how many man-years of computation it could perform in some unbelievably short time. Business seldom deals with mathematics more complex than addition and subtraction, but there is always a need to store the numbers that are involved, to sort them in different ways, and to print them out in readable formats. Business software, then, deals primarily with the *storage* of data (both numbers and words), and with *retrieving* the information at a later time.

DATA GENERATION AND STORAGE

One of the most useful features of a computer is its ability to store information for later retrieval. Nearly all business software depends on this one feature; both magnetic disk and magnetic tape have been widely used for this purpose. Magnetic media of some kind are a necessity, as they can retain information indefinitely outside of the computer. Such storage casts the computer in the role of a file cabinet.

In all but the simplest programs, information is either entered by the operator, generated by the machine, or both. In many instances, if not most, there is a need to provide more-or-less permanent storage of some part of the information thus generated. An example program later in this chapter deals with a check register, a rather simple and typical real-life case of what we are discussing. In a manual check register, the object is to record each transaction by adding *deposits* and subtracting *checks* and *bank charges*. The simple arithmetic of balancing the account is trivial by computer standards, or even human standards, if the data are all available. The automated checkbook is, therefore, mostly a case of storing and retrieving data, which in this example just happen to be bank transactions.

It will also be demonstrated in the following pages that the retrieved information need not be in the same format as entered. When the computer recovers and/or prints the stored data in a form other than as originally entered, it can be said to have *sorted* or *formatted* the information. Whether the information is considered to be sorted or formatted depends on the purpose for which it has been retrieved. To some extent, then, the computer system can be considered to have functioned in the role of both the filing system and the clerk that organizes, files, and later retrieves the information. With this in mind, the method of storage should be reviewed briefly

HOW DATA IS STORED

For the modern small business, data storage and recovery mean getting data onto, and later from, the floppy disk. The user should realize that this is a rather complex procedure that nevertheless requires very little effort on his or her part. It is one of the procedures taken care of by the operating system mentioned briefly in an earlier chapter. It is necessary for the programmer to insert the right commands in the program, and for the operator to make the correct responses to "prompts" (messages) appearing on the screen from time to time. The same procedures apply to reading the data later.

Example 5-1 is excerpted from the "CHECKING" program. Line 1400 is a typical "read the file" statement, and line 1580 is a typical "write the file" statement. These lines occur at different points in the program, and are grouped together here only for illustration.

Example 5-1. Read/Write Disk-Addressing Commands

```
1400 READ #1%Y*64, E, N, D$, I$, C, D, B
1580 WRITE #1%E*64, E, N, D$, I$, C, D, B
```

Example 5-1 is in North Star BASIC. The North Star operating system calculates the disk address as 64 (bytes) times E (the file number or record number that is being processed). The variables, E, N, D$, I$, C, D, and B, make up one complete record, the data for which the operator has just entered. The read statement is identical, except that the record number has been expressed as Y. If E and Y are equal, the two statements will be applicable to exactly the same disk address. Notice that E is also a part of the stored record in this instance; it need not be when space is at a premium.

It should be noted that other BASICs may require significantly different statements to achieve the same purpose.

DISK HANDLING

The part of the whole operation that is controlled by humans—the insertion, removal, and storage of the diskettes—does require some care. Diskettes are unbelievably long-lived if handled carefully, but the programmer has not yet been born who has never ruined a disk by some sort of mistake or accident.

Since the disk has a magnetic surface, it must be stored and kept away from magnetic fields. As a flexible device, the disk must not be bent, creased, or exposed to stresses and strains lest it be scratched or otherwise weakened. Most importantly, it must be kept clean; an ordinary audio tape or record can pick up a lot of noise and still be usable, but the computer may completely reject a diskette, which has your entire inventory on it, because of "noisy" spots caused by dust, scratches, or oily fingerprints. Or, worse yet, the computer will read the disk in a faulty manner. Another important point is that there should be no smoking in the room housing the computer and its diskettes. Extremes of temperature and humidity should also be avoided.

THE DISK LIBRARY

Another responsibility of the human operator is to implement a *library function* for the diskettes. Diskettes are removable media and even the smallest operation will soon find itself with several disks on hand, perhaps dozens. In addition to being carefully stored, they must be labeled and cataloged in some manner. Each diskette will contain a machine-readable directory of the file names upon it, which the operating system can print at the operator's request. It is more convenient, however, to somehow indicate the contents on the jacket so that the operator can identify the contents without having to put the disk in the computer. Labels are nearly always provided for this purpose. A payroll disk containing half a dozen programs and two or three data files might simply be identified as "Payroll 1," perhaps with the beginning and ending dates for the information on the disk.

An equally important library function is the maintenance of *backup* disks. Diskettes containing the *operating software* must especially be protected by making an initial backup copy and then, if no actual programs are to be placed on the working copy, protecting it, too, from accidentally being written on. The way in which this is done varies with different hardware systems. A backup copy of each program must also exist, as must a fairly up-to-date copy of data files.

One of the most common methods of doing this is to place a program set (such as the payroll) on the same diskette as the associated data files. Then each week (or each day if there is much activity in the files) make a backup copy of the entire diskette. Next, the original known-good diskette is saved as a backup, and the copy is used the following day. The two diskettes would then be swapped on a daily basis and, in case of catastrophe, only one day's operation need be reconstructed.

With these precautions in mind, our example will continue with the construction of a check-register program, mainly to illustrate the storage and later retrieval of business information. A program of this kind might also be made a part of a payroll or similar package when checks need to be generated and/or accounted for by program activity.

FILE STRUCTURE

The smallest useful division of a data file is the field. A number, letter, symbol, word, or string of words can all be fields. In the checkbook, the check number will be a field, the date will be a field, and the deposit will be a field, as will the description or reason for the check. Example 5-2 shows a typical entry that might be made in a check register.

Example 5-2. An Example of a Checkbook Entry

101   11/7/1980   PAY ELECTRIC BILL   23.00   00.00   98.57

In this record, 101 is the check number. The next field is the date, followed by the description. The check number is a numeric variable and the next two fields are string variables. String variables can contain characters other than numbers. Following that we have the amount of the check, a column for the deposit, if any, and the balance. In BASIC, these fields might be listed as N, D$, I$, C, D, and B. Again, in BASIC, the balance, B, can be calculated by the program as $B = D - C$, and need not be stored in the file. This is similar to the way it will be done in our example program. (In Program Listing 5-1, the balance is carried forward in the file, so that reading the register does not always have to begin at entry number one.) But the main purpose of this kind of program is not calculation, but mere storage and retrieval of the records.

Program Listing 5–1. "CHECKING"

```
1000 REM PROGRAM CHECKING -- NORTH STAR BASIC REL.4
1010 DIM I$(15)\REM FIELD FOR ITEM DESCRIPTION
1020 E2=100\REM NUMBER OF ENTRIES TO BE MADE
1030 PRINT CHR$(12)\REM PLACE CLEAR SCREEN CHAR HERE
1040 PRINT"CHECKING ACCOUNT"
1050 PRINT"****************"
1060 PRINT
1070 PRINT"1) MAKE A CHECKBOOK ENTRY"
1080 PRINT"2) READ THE ENTRIES"
1090 PRINT"3) CREATE A NEW FILE"\PRINT
1100 INPUT"SELECT BY NUMBER",Q
1110 IF Q<1 OR Q>4 OR Q<>INT(Q) THEN 1100
1120 ON Q GOTO 1130,1300,1500
1130 GOSUB 1540\REM GET CURRENT BALANCE
1140 E1=E\PRINT
1150 PRINT"LAST ENTRY:"\GOSUB 1440\REM TO DISPLAY IT
1160 B1=B\REM BALANCE FORWARD
1170 INPUT"CHECK NUMBER      :",N
1180 INPUT"DATE  AS mm/dd/yy :",D$
1190 IF LEN(D$)>8 THEN 1180
1200 INPUT"DESCRIPTION       :",I$
1210 IF LEN(I$)>15 THEN I$=I$(1,15)\C=0\D=0
1220 INPUT"AMOUNT            :",A
1230 IF N>0 THEN C=A*(-1)
1240 IF N=0 THEN D=A\B=B1+C+D
1250 E=E1+1\GOSUB 1440
1260 INPUT"APPROVED (Y/N)",Q$\IF Q$<>"Y" THEN 1170
1270 GOSUB 1560\REM FILE IT
1280 CLOSE#1\GOTO 1030
1290 REM TO READ AND PRINT
1300 GOSUB 1540\REM READ LAST ENTRY
1310 INPUT"START AT CHECK #: ",Q
1320 IF Q<0 OR Q>E1 OR Q<>INT(Q) THEN 1300
1330 E1=E
1340 FOR X=1 TO E1
1350     READ#1%X*64,E,N
1360     IF N<>Q THEN 1380
1370     EXIT 1390
1380 NEXT X
1390 FOR Y=X TO E1
1400     READ#1%Y*64,E,N,D$,I$,C,D,B
1410     GOSUB 1470\REM PRINT IT
1420 NEXT Y\CLOSE#1\GOTO 1030
1430 REM DISPLAY ROUTINE
1440 PRINT\PRINT"ENTRY# ",E," CK#",N," ",D$," ",I$,%8F2,C,D,B
1450 RETURN
1460 REM LISTING ROUTINE
1470 PRINT#1,"ENTRY#",E," CK#",N," ",D$," ",I$,
1480 PRINT#1,TAB(40),%9F2,C,D,B,CHR$(10)\RETURN
1490 REM CREATE FILE ROUTINE
1500 CREATE"REGISTER",INT(1+E2/4)
1510 OPEN#1,"REGISTER"\WRITE#1%0,0,0," "," ",0,0,0
1520 CLOSE#1\GOTO 1030
1530 REM READ AN ENTRY
1540 OPEN#1,"REGISTER"\READ #1%0,E,N,D$,I$,C,D,B\RETURN
1550 REM UPDATE"LAST RECORD"
1560 WRITE#1%0,E,N,D$,I$,C,D,B
1570 REM WRITE CURRENT ENTRY
1580 WRITE#1%E*64,E,N,D$,I$,C,D,B\RETURN
```

The individual fields are combined to make up a record; that is, all of the pertinent information for a single transaction. Any number of records may be combined to make up a file; in this case, a data file analogous to a checkbook. Can a program be made to actually print the check itself? The answer is yes; large payroll programs (see Chapter 7) often do this. Printing checks by computer requires checks and stubs that have been printed on forms that can be accepted by your computer's printer, and it is hardly worthwhile unless many checks are to be printed, or unless a separate, small printer can be devoted full time to this purpose.

OVERVIEW OF "CHECKING" PROGRAM

Fig. 4–2 (in the previous chapter) is the system diagram of a program to record checking transactions and print out the register when desired. This kind of diagram is interpreted as representing a program, a keyboard for input, and some means of printed output. Although the print symbol usually means "on paper" it can also represent a crt display. The symbol for a disk file is shown connected to the program. This is a simple example of system diagramming.

Fig. 5–1 is the flowchart of the same program, with explanatory notes which should make clear the flow of control and the essentials of how it all goes together. The program can be outlined in English as follows:

1. Open the check file and read the last entry.
2. Input, via the operator keyboard, the choice of reading and printing, or entering new data.
3. If the instruction is to read and print the register, read and print the entire file. (Note: There should be an option to begin reading at some point other than the first recorded entry.)
4. If the choice is to make an entry, input the pertinent information via the keyboard.
5. If the entry is correct, write it in the file. If it is in error, reenter the data.
6. If further entries are desired, repeat Steps 2 through 5.
7. When finished, close the file and exit the program.

This sort of program makes use of very few mathematical manipulations. The operator is asked to input a check number for each entry. If the number is zero, the program assumes a deposit is taking place and stores the dollar amount in the deposit field, then adds it to the previous balance. If the check number is greater than zero, a valid check is assumed, and the amount will be treated as a check and subtracted from the previous balance. The only exceptions to this rule are bank charges, which must be entered with a check number of zero. To prevent these being considered deposits, they are entered with a minus

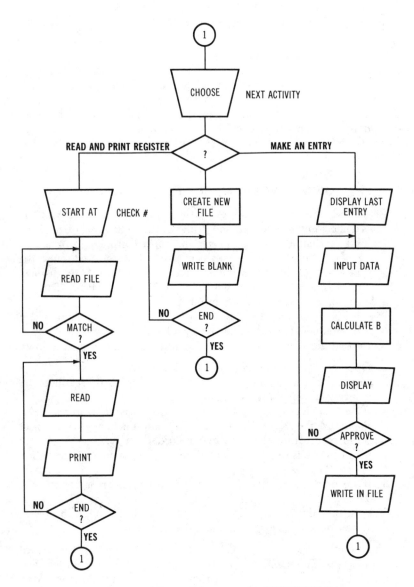

Fig. 5-1. Flowchart of the program, "CHECKING."

sign. The latest balance is generated by adding together the previous balance, the deposit (if any), and the check amount, which will always be a negative number.

The technique just mentioned makes use of the computer's ability to "make a decision" based on the data itself (the check numbers and the amounts that were input). This will be done by means of the IF-THEN statement, which is universal in BASIC. The program will have been written so that IF the check number is greater than zero, THEN the amount will be multiplied by minus one. This is illustrated in Example 5–3.

Example 5–3. A Checking Calculation

```
1000 IF N > 0 THEN A = A* (−1)
```

In this example, 1000 is the line number, N is the check number, and A is the amount. This changes the sign of A, the figure you input, if N is a number greater than zero. If N is zero, and the amount is entered as a negative number, the resulting A is a positive number. Example 5–4 shows the calculation of the new balance.

Example 5–4. A Balance Calculation

```
1010 B = B1 + D + C
```

This example adds the previous balance, the check, and the deposit to yield the new balance. Here, C (check) is a minus number, so adding it to B1 (old balance) is the same as a subtraction. Fig. 5–2 illustrates a typical output from "CHECKING."

The checkbook example should be clearly understood before proceeding to later chapters, as the same storage and retrieval techniques will be found to be part of many succeeding examples. Nearly all business software will contain a minimum of one data file, the program(s) for making entries and corrections and for listing or editing the file, and some means, often yet another program, for making use of the stored data. This will be true of the inventory, payroll, and general ledger programs described in later chapters. By having this fundamental technique fully understood, the reader will have a head start toward understanding those more complicated packages.

SORTING COMPUTER DATA

Sorting is one of the most common kinds of manipulations that are applied to data. A list of names and addresses, for example, will normally

```
ENTRY# 1 CK# 0 10/21/79 FIRST DEPOSIT      .00   300.00   300.00
ENTRY# 2 CK# 1 10/22/79 PAY THE RENT   -210.00      .00    90.00
ENTRY# 3 CK# 2 11/01/79 PETTY CASH      -25.00      .00    65.00
ENTRY# 4 CK# 0 11/09/79 DEPOSIT           .00   212.32   277.32
ENTRY# 5 CK# 3 11/10/79 PHONE BILL      -63.45      .00   213.87
```

Fig. 5-2. Sample printout of the program, "CHECKING."

be most useful if it is kept in alphabetical order. (Imagine looking for a phone number in an unsorted list of telephone customers.) Sorting may also be by number, in either ascending or descending order, and sometimes a combination of these two forms may be used.

Another kind of sorting, more properly referred to as *ordering*, is widely used in computer programs. Ordering consists of grouping like items, such as a number of transactions that all occurred in the same day or the same month. Sorting and ordering are among the most common ways of manipulating business information. Sorting, or ordering, may be accomplished at the time the data enters the system, or at the time it is retrieved for some particular use. In many instances, the stored data is to be used for more than one purpose; obviously, then, there is little need to sort it until it is to be used, as the same data may be needed, when finally printed, in several different formats. Example programs in this book will demonstrate both general methods; that is, sorting at the time of entry and at the time of printing.

Assume for a moment that the program just discussed had dealt with names and addresses rather than checkbook entries. Names and addresses would have been entered more or less at random, without regard for alphabetical order. At some future time, the operator might wish to print the entire file in ascending order, A through Z, to enable quicker location of a particular record.

Such a program would follow almost exactly the same methods as did the checking program. There would be one additional section, a "sort routine" of some kind. There are many ways a computer can sort such a list and they will not be dealt with in detail at this time. The point to be made is that storage and retrieval are about the same in all cases; such details as figuring dollar balances, or alphabetical sorting, useful as these features might be, are simply side issues to the main program flow.

When sorting is a necessity, it usually involves one of the following methods, and any of several sorting techniques, which are covered in detail in books devoted to that subject alone.

1. By *numerical order*, either ascending or descending. A common use of this method is to sort a chart of accounts such as the one that will be described in Chapter 8.
2. In *alphabetical order*, as in the case of a name-and-address list to be presented in this chapter.

Alphabetical sorting can deal with the entire "key field" or with just a portion of it. In our mailing list example, the names will be sorted by the first letter of the last name. In that technique, the name Jones is treated, for sorting, as if it were only the letter "J." James might follow Jones in the list, but at least all the J names would be grouped together.

The *ASCII code* for the numbers, letters, and punctuation marks, which we can input to a keyboard, consists of a numerical representation for each such character. The code for B is larger than that for A, and so on through the alphabet; thus, if the ASCII A and the ASCII B are compared by their numerical value, A will come before B. To sort by the first letter in the name, the letters are converted to numbers, and then sorted by number. The numbers are used internally by the sort routine, and the process is transparent to the operator.

By a slight change in method (involving more program detail and some loss of speed) true alphabetical order can be achieved. Space consuming string arrays are used, and each entire name is compared with another, letter by letter. In our program, we use the ASCII value of the first letter only. The name whose first letter has the lowest numeric value is placed below the other. By doing this repeatedly the entire list will eventually be put in approximate alphabetical order.

Fig. 5–3 is the flowchart for a mailing-list program in which names are sorted in the manner just described. Program Listing 5–2 is the BASIC program for accomplishing this purpose. Both the flowchart and listing will be referred to as the program is being analyzed.

The program, "NAMELIST," stores and retrieves information much as the checking program did (and as nearly all business software does to some extent). Besides simple storage and retrieval, it permits printing in two different formats—the line for making long lists, and the label format for printing labels. It also permits display on the video screen in either format for quick access, and will find all listings for a particular last name that may be input for comparison. The feature for which it is included in this chapter, however, is to illustrate the principle of sorting. This principle will also be discussed in later chapters. At this time it should be noted that the sort method used in this program is not the best or worst of such methods. It is reasonably fast and adequate for the intended purpose.

PROGRAM ANALYSIS—"NAMELIST"

This program opens, as do most business programs, with an introductory portion that sets the stage for the real activity. A "menu" is printed on the screen of the terminal, and the operator is "prompted" to choose an activity. Prior to the menu, but as part of the same section, the program has opened the data file and read the last entry so that it "knows" where, in the disk file, the next entry is to be stored. After making his or her choice, the operator is offered the option of printing on the screen or on the printer by setting the value of the variable, U. The use of this feature will be explained a little later. The program is now ready for whatever activity the operator has chosen. All of these preliminary functions have taken place under the direction of lines 1000–1140.

Lines 1150 and 1160, together with subroutine 1920, take care of the

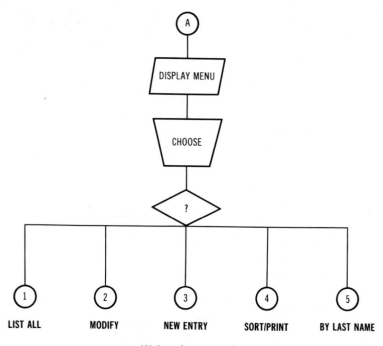

(A) Introductory portion.

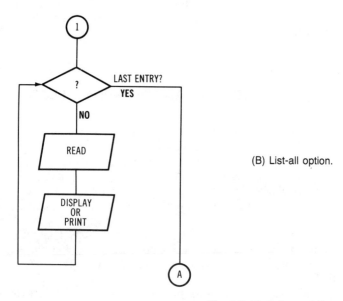

(B) List-all option.

Fig. 5-3. Flowchart of the

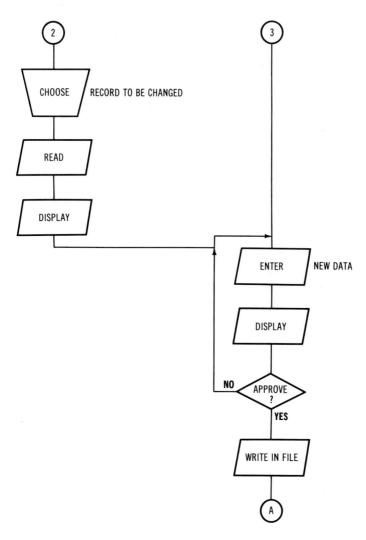

(C) New-entries-and-changes option.

program, "NAMELIST."

Continued on next page

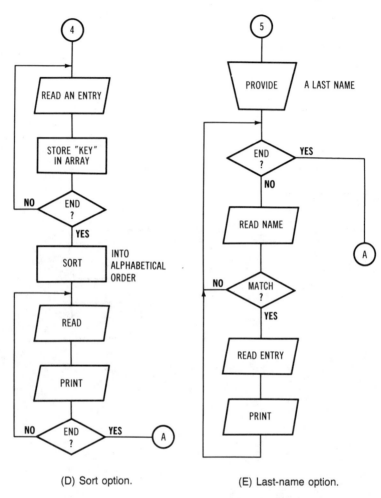

(D) Sort option.

(E) Last-name option.

Fig. 5-3. Flowchart of the program, "NAMELIST" (cont).

first option, which is to *print the entire file* in the order in which the names and addresses were originally entered in the file. This is an unsorted list. Subroutine 1920, which both reads the file and prints the list, may be considered a typical *file read-and-print* operation as it is accomplished by North Star BASIC.

File handling is one of the major points of difference between various BASICs. Line 1920 illustrates the way in which a file is read in this dialect. The READ#1 statement is the program's instruction to read from file number 1, which is the number assigned when the file,

Program Listing 5–2. "NAMELIST"

```
1000 REM PROGRAM 'NAMELIST'****VERS 78.2*****NORTH STAR REL 4
1010 DIM A$(16),A1$(15),N$(10),N1$(12),T$(12)
1020 REM OPEN FILE AND DETERMINE FILE LENGTH
1030 OPEN #1,"NAMES"
1040 READ#1%0,A\Z=A\A=0
1045 REM
1050 PRINT"1. LIST ENTIRE FILE"\PRINT"2. MODIFY A RECORD"
1060 PRINT"3. NEW ENTRY"\PRINT"4. SORTED LIST"
1070 PRINT"5. FIND BY LAST NAME"\PRINT
1080 PRINT "SELECT BY NUMBER",
1090 REM
1100 INPUT Q\IF Q<1 OR Q>5 OR Q<>INT(Q) THEN 1080
1110 IF Q<>2 AND Q<>3 THEN 1120 ELSE 1140
1120 PRINT"INPUT P FOR PRINT, V FOR VIDEO",\INPUT Q$
1130 IF Q$="P" THEN U=1 ELSE U=0
1140 ON Q GOTO 1150,1170,1200,1470,1860
1150 A=A+1\IF A>Z THEN 1040 ELSE GOSUB 1920
1160 GOTO 1150
1170 INPUT"#: ",A\IF A>Z THEN 1050
1180 GOSUB 2060
1190 GOTO 1230
1200 A=Z+1\REM INCREMENT RECORD COUNTER
1210 REM
1220 REM DISPLAY FOR ENTRY
1230 PRINTTAB(20),"#",A\ON Q GOTO 1240,1240,1360
1240 PRINTTAB(20),"1.",N$\ON Q GOTO 1250,1250,1370
1250 PRINTTAB(20),"2.",N1$
1260 PRINTTAB(20),"3.",A$
1270 PRINTTAB(20), "4.",A1$
1280 PRINTTAB(20),"5.",Z$
1290 PRINTTAB(20),"6.",T$
1300 PRINT
1310 PRINTTAB(20),"7. FILE IT AS IS "
1320 INPUT"LINE #? ",Q1
1330 ON Q1 GOTO 1360,1370,1380,1390,1400,1410,1420
1340 REM
1350 REM INPUT THE VALUES
1360 INPUT"LAST NAME:",N$\IF Q=2 THEN 1230
1370 INPUT"FIRST    :",N1$\IF Q=2 THEN 1230
1380 INPUT"ADDRESS  :",A$\IF Q=2 THEN 1230
1390 INPUT"CITYSTATE:",A1$\IF Q=2 THEN 1230
1400 INPUT"ZIP      :",Z$\IF Q=2 THEN 1230
1410 INPUT"PHONE    :",T$\IF Q=2 THEN 1230
1420 GOSUB 2020
1430 IF Q=3 THEN GOSUB 2040
1440 CLOSE #1\PRINT"FILED ON DISK"
1450 GOTO 1030
1460 REM
1470 REM SORT ROUTINE BEGINS HERE
1480 REM START BY SETTING ARRAYS
1490 REM CONVERT FIRST LETTER TO ASCII VALUE
1500 REM FOR NUMERIC SORT
```

Program Listing 5–2 (cont)

```
1510 Q=0  \READ #1%Q,A\N=A
1520 DIM X(N),X1(N)
1530 FOR I=1 TO N
1540 Q=Q+100\IF Q>N*100 THEN EXIT 1730
1550 READ#1%Q,A,N$
1560 X1(I)=A\X (I)=ASC(N$)\REM LETTER BECOMES NUMBER
1570 NEXT I
1580 ! "     SORTING......."
1590 M=N
1600 M=INT(M/2)
1610 IF M=0 THEN 1800
1620 J=1
1630 K=N-M
1640 I=J
1650 L=I+M
1660 IF X(I)<X(L) THEN 1770
1670 !"S",
1680 T=X(I)
1690 T1=X1(I)
1700 X(I)=X(L)
1710 X1(I)=X1(L)
1720 X(L)=T
1730 X1(L)=T1
1740 I=I-M
1750 IF I<1 THEN 1770
1760 GOTO 1650
1770 J=J+1
1780 IF J>K THEN 1600
1790 GOTO 1630
1800 !".....SORTED....."\GOSUB 2000
1810 FOR I=1 TO N
1820 A=X1(I)
1830 GOSUB 1920
1840 NEXT I
1850 GOTO 1040
1860 INPUT"LAST NAME:",N9$\A=1
1870 IF A>Z THEN 1040
1880 READ#1%A*100,A,N$
1890 IF N$=N9$ THEN GOSUB 1960
1900 A=A+1
1910 GOTO 1870
1920 READ#1%A*     100,A,N$,N1$,A$,A1$,Z$,T$\REM PRINT IN-LINE
1930 !#U,A,TAB(4),N$,",",N1$, TAB(26),T$,TAB(39),A$
1940 !#U,TAB(39),A1$,TAB(55),Z$\RETURN
1950 REM
1960 READ#1%A*100,A,N$,N1$,A$,A1$,Z$,T$\!\REM READ AND PRINT
1970 PRINT#U,A,TAB(4),N$," ",N1$,TAB(30),T$
1980 PRINT#U,TAB(4),A$                \REM PRINT AS A LABEL
1990 PRINT#U,TAB(4),A1$," ",Z$
2000 PRINT#U,CHR$(10)\RETURN
2010 REM
2020 WRITE#1%A*100,A,N$,N1$,A$,A1$,Z$,T$\RETURN\REM WRITE FILE
2030 REM
2040 WRITE#1%0,A\RETURN\REM UPDATE EOF INDICATOR
2050 REM
2060 READ#1%A*100,A,N$,N1$,A$,A1$,Z$,T$\RETURN\REM READ ONLY
```

NAMES, was declared in the opening lines of the program. This BASIC dialect addresses files by *byte number* when used in this (random access) mode. A record length of 100 bytes is used for each record even though some may not require the full length. A is a variable which represents the record number; that is, the first record entered was 1 and record 100 is the hundredth record in this particular file.

The syntax for describing a particular address, in this instance, is %A*100. In this version of BASIC, the percent sign, when used in a file statement, indicates that a calculated file address follows. The entire statement, READ#1%A*100, means that record 1 will be found at the 100th byte in file number 1, record 2 at the 200th byte, and so on. Notice that this numbering system leaves one blank record, record 0, at the beginning of the file. It will be used for a slightly different purpose than the other records.

The remainder of the file-read statement names the variables that are to be read from the record. The operating system used with this dialect of BASIC marks each field in the record in a way that identifies it as either a numeric or a string variable. The variables are entered in the same order in each record and, therefore, any record in this particular file can be read with the same READ instruction by changing only the record number.

The PRINT statement, lines 1930 and 1940, prints the fields in a readable manner. The exclamation point is North Star "shorthand" for the PRINT instruction. North Star allows printing by *device number;* that is, peripheral device #0 is the console, #1 is the printer, and other numbers can be assigned to other peripheral devices. This method of addressing peripherals allows one to "print" at a particular device, as determined by the value of a variable, such as the letter U used in this program. At various points in the program, you can change the value of U and thereby cause the program output to go to either the video screen or the printer. In other BASICs, different methods are used, some of them much less flexible.

Entries and Changes

Lines 1170–1460 deal with making entries and correcting existing entries. A correction might be made, for example, if one of the entities in the name and address list has had a change of address or telephone number. The two activities differ from one another mainly in that for a new entry the program assigns the file address (line 1200) and for changes, the operator calls for the old record by number (line 1170).

Printing a Sorted List

This program has been introduced to demonstrate one kind of sorting activity. The file itself is not sorted in this instance, but the printed output is, if this option is chosen by the operator. Look ahead to lines 1810–1840 and notice that the mechanism for this print option is a short and simple loop which, along with subroutine 1920, reads and prints the entire file. This is almost the same thing that was done when printing the unsorted file. The major difference is that the unsorted list was read from the file in order of address; that is, record 1, 2, 3, and so on, while this printed list will be read by alphabetical order of the names.

Lines 1470–1800 make up the sort routine. This routine first reads record 0 to determine the length of the file, then dimensions two arrays (line 1520) which are the length of the file—a 100-record file will result in arrays dimensioned as $X(100)$ and $X1(100)$. It should be noted that some BASICs do not permit the dimensioning of arrays in the body of the program. These arrays will be used as the basis for sorting, and later printing, the file's records. Lines 1530–1570 make up a loop, which reads the last names from the file in the order in which they were written, converts the first letter of the last names to their ASCII (numeric) values, and stores them in array X. At the same time, the record numbers are stored in the corresponding cells of array $X1$.

This routine is based on a general type of sorting called the *Shell* sort. It works by dividing the list to be sorted, comparing pairs of values and rearranging them, and redividing the list until the numbers are in ascending order. In this example, the list of numbers represents file records. As the "keys," or ASCII representations of the names are reordered, so are their accompanying record numbers in the corresponding array. Lines 1660–1670 make the exchanges each time that a wrong order is detected, and the final result is that array $X1$ contains the file addresses arranged in the order dictated by the record's contents; in this case, the alphabetical order of the last names. This method of sorting is midway between the slower and faster methods of sorting and is short and simple enough to be incorporated into most small programs.

Summary of Program "NAMELIST"

We have discussed the printing of this list by the order in which the names were entered, and in a sorted order by last names. If it is desired to sort by zip code or by telephone exchange, similar methods can be used. The remaining features of the program can be described briefly: The file can be searched to locate a particular name (lines 1860–1910), and there are two optional print formats—the one used for lists and a second format that will fit a mailing label.

There are more refined methods that the reader is encouraged to investigate after learning the simpler techniques. A classic work on "sorting and searching" is listed at the end of the chapter.[2] The more exotic methods of storing and retrieving information involve rather complicated algorithms which are worthwhile mastering if a great deal of data is to be handled. For small files, these methods have only academic interest. Fig. 5–4 illustrates typical printer outputs for the "NAMELIST" program.

```
1   KAUFMAN,W.T          NO PHONE    R.R.12
                                     KILA, MT        59999

2   SCHUMAN,ERNEST       NO PHONE    12347 4TH AVE
                                     SMALLTOWN, TX   75000

3   FRANKLIN,WILLIAM     NO PHONE    GENERAL DELIVERY
                                     DUBOIS, ID      78654

4   ELECTRONIC,LTD       SKY-9876    MAIN STREET
                                     CALGARY ALB.    NO ZIP

5   COMLABS,INC          406-257-0436 BOX 1082
                                      KALISPELL,MT   59901
```

(A) A list of names and addresses as entered.

```
5   COMLABS,INC          406-257-0436 BOX 1082
                                      KALISPELL,MT   59901

4   ELECTRONIC,LTD       SKY-9876    MAIN STREET
                                     CALGARY ALB.    NO ZIP

3   FRANKLIN,WILLIAM     NO PHONE    GENERAL DELIVERY
                                     DUBOIS, ID      78654

1   KAUFMAN,W.T          NO PHONE    R.R.12
                                     KILA, MT        59999

2   SCHUMAN,ERNEST       NO PHONE    12347 4TH AVE
                                     SMALLTOWN, TX   75000
```

(B) A list of names and addresses after sorting.

```
3   FRANKLIN,WILLIAM
    GENERAL DELIVERY
    DUBOIS, ID 78654
```

(C) A name and address printed as a label.

Fig. 5–4. Sample printouts of the program, "NAMELIST."

SELF-HELP TEST QUESTIONS

1. Why are backup disks kept?

2. How do you prevent damage to stored disks?

3. Define the following:
   (a) A field.
   (b) A record.
   (c) A file.

4. How can a computer rearrange stored data?

5. How common is storage and retrieval in business software?

REFERENCES

1. Coan, J.S. *Basic BASIC*, 2nd ed. Hayden Book Co., Inc., Rochelle Park, NJ, 1978.

2. Knuth, D.E. *The Art of Computer Programming. Volume 3: Sorting and Searching.* Addison-Wesley Publishing Co., Inc., Reading, MA, 1973.

6

Inventory Control

OBJECTIVES

After studying this chapter, you should be familiar with the following:

- When an inventory is needed.
- What an inventory should contain.
- Any benefits a computer inventory can offer.
- How to go about writing and evaluating inventory programs.

All of us have some things we keep track of even if they are only our personal possessions. Having the up-to-date information on such collections, if they represent much in time and/or money, constitutes *inventory control*. In a somewhat broader sense, inventory control is the entire management process that handles inventory decisions. Any contributions by the computer that may simplify the process can be considered valuable to the business.

WHO NEEDS AN INVENTORY?

If the need for a business inventory exists, the owner need look no further for the justification for a computer. Those who can keep their inventory on the back of an old envelope may not find it economically sound. This chapter, then, is for those who deal in larger numbers, or who anticipate rapid turnover or frequent price changes, or who are concerned about lost interest on nonworking capital. Most of all, this chapter applies to the business person or programmer who has the need for a computer to manage an inventory, whether the computer and the software are to be purchased as a "turnkey" system, or put together piece by piece. In either case, the business person or programmer must know where to begin.

INVENTORY AS A LIST

An inventory begins as just a list and as such it resembles very much the earlier examples of information storage and retrieval. In addition, though, the retrieval will be more selective and there will be more interest in the costs of the inventoried products and in certain other special fields, such as part numbers, replacement codes, and so on, that will be added. These additions change the simple list into an *inventory system*.

As we begin this exercise it is advisable to have at hand some graph paper with squares large enough to write in, on which a sample list may be constructed. The divided squares will make it easier to determine the spacing of the information. At this point, a few items will be listed in the same manner as they will eventually appear on your computer printout. You must be consistent and logical. A description of the article will be required, as will the cost and the number on hand. This is probably the absolute minimum. If many articles are to be involved, a unique part number will be required. One manufacturer of thousands of different types of transistors assigns a number, such as 48 99999, to each different type. In this case, the 48 stands for solid-state device, and the complete number is unique to only one type of transistor. Our list of parts might begin, then, with an entry such as is shown in Example 6–1.

Example 6–1. Sample Inventory Entry for a Transistor

QTY	CODE-NUMBER	DESCRIPTION	PRICE	TOTAL
3	48 99999	TRANSISTOR	0.79	2.37

The last column is the unit price times the quantity on hand. Note that the total value can be calculated anew each time the record is printed, and need not be a permanent part of the *stored data*. As several thousand records may be involved, this technique saves a great deal of storage space on the disk.

We might expand on this sample record by setting some minimum quantity we would like to have on hand, and it would be helpful to know if any more are on order. These two items can be added to the record as in Example 6–2.

Example 6–2. Sample Inventory Entry With the Addition of Ordering and Minimum Quantity Information

ORD	MIN	QTY	CODE-NUMBER	DESCRIPTION	PRICE	TOTAL
2	5	3	48 99999	TRANSISTOR	0.79	2.37

The new figures are meant to indicate that a minimum level of five is required and that there are two on order. To the preceding inventory record any number of additional items of information may be added, keeping in mind that *as the record grows longer, fewer of them can fit in your memory devices*. As a practical compromise, five to eight items can be included for each record, although some elaborate systems provide details such as the name and address of the supplier for each part. (One very practical inventory control system actually prints the sales ticket, removes the merchandise from the inventory count, and generates, if necessary, a reorder. Although this is very convenient, it is a bit too much to expect from a really small system.)

Two more fields, though, will be of use to nearly every inventory program. These are the file address (disk address) and the date of last activity, such as a sale, removal, or reorder. Only the date needs to be part of the file record, and it can be added automatically to each entry by the program. The disk address (exact location on the disk occupied by a specific record) can also be calculated by the program for both reading and writing operations, and can be printed as another form of identification. (In the example program the disk address, or record number, is stored within the record although it does not have to be if space is at a premium.)

The file record as it has just been described may be printed as in Example 6–3.

Example 6–3. A Printed Inventory File Record

FILE-DATE	ORD-MIN-QTY			CODE-NUMBER	DESCRIPTION	PRICE	TOTAL
1 10.80	2	5	3	48 99999	TRANSISTOR	0.79	2.37

The three quantities will be numbers, stored as part of the record. In this program they are all "packed" into one variable to save file space. The price and date will also be stored numbers. The identification (stock or serial number) and description will be stored as string variables, as they may contain characters other than numbers. The "TOTAL" field will be calculated at print time. A few other items may be added to these samples when we get into the actual program.

The first field, "FILE," is the disk address mentioned earlier. This example is for record number 1. It will be found at the first storage space in the data file. Calculating file addresses is a matter of much variation when one version of BASIC is compared to others. Where rapid access to records is desired, so-called "random-access" methods are used. As contrasted with sequential access in which the entire file must be read to find any one record, random access enables the program to go immediately to any position in the file. It is, therefore, the fastest method of locating a record.

The file address is determined by the program at the time the record is first written on the disk, and is a function of the record length and the particular disk operating system involved. Because of the kind of BASIC the example program uses, the file addresses are based on 128-byte sectors numbered from 1 upward, which must be divided by the addressing technique into fractional addresses. In this version of BASIC, records should be a multiple of the sectors, or an even division of the sector, such as 2, 4, or 8 subrecords. Dividing the sector-length records into thirds, as is done in the example program, is rather clumsy but it is done to make most efficient use of the file space.

Although the fields within the record are referred to as being numeric and string variables, it should be noted that this particular version of BASIC stores everything as strings, converting the numeric fields back to numeric values when they are to be accessed or manipulated in any way other than for file storage. This can be considered either good or bad, depending on your viewpoint. It saves a few bytes of space, but it requires more complicated methods of assigning the variables to fields.

If a symbol is used to indicate special orders, it may also be printed, and in some cases the manufacturer's name or a code to represent it may be necessary. In this program there is a 2-character field for a user-assigned code and a double asterisk (**) to indicate that a record is special in some way; for example, that it is a special order or that it is to be handled differently than the other merchandise.

Another refinement is to indicate the unit of measure for the quantities; that is, dozen, gross, or each. There is a 2-character field for this in the sample program. The sample program is adequate for many purposes and will serve to illustrate the principles of an inventory control program. If many more fields are required to adequately describe or control the merchandise, a wider printed page will be needed, and many small systems will not accommodate the larger paper.

INVENTORY FUNCTIONS

The example inventory program will provide for three different kinds of activity: (1) making entries in the file, (2) making changes to entries as needed, and (3) printing the entire file or any part of it. It is this last activity that requires the most attention; the entries themselves are just another form of our old friend, data storage. The retrieval, in the case of inventory, can become as complicated as the user wishes it to be. It may be useful to retrieve an entry, for example, by any of the following fields:

1. The part number.
2. The file address.
3. Classification by type or manufacturer.
4. All those with outstanding orders.
5. All those below the minimum level.
6. Those having no activity for, say, six months.

It also may be helpful, at tax time, to run a total on the value of all merchandise in stock, based on the latest prices.

The three separate functions—entries, corrections, and retrieval—may be combined in one long program, if desired. It is usually simpler and less demanding on the small machine's memory to divide the functions among two or more programs. The example program (Program Listing 6–1) combines all of the functions; it occupies slightly over 14K bytes of memory, which is nearly all of the available memory in typical small computers. A smaller memory or a larger program would demand that the functions of the system be divided in some manner. This is generally true of many small-business software packages. The example program was originally two smaller programs, one for making entries and corrections (functions very much alike), and the other to handle information retrieval and listings.

Entries

When the inventory system is placed in operation for the first time, and when new merchandise is added to stock, the information must be entered into the file. If the operator has chosen to make entries, the program automatically assigns to that entry the *next available unused file address*. This is an automatic function which is nearly universal in disk-based business software. There are two ways of accomplishing this function. With one method, the empty file is "initialized" before use by writing a minus number (or some program-recognizable character) in every available record space. This method is demonstrated by the chart-of-accounts program, "ACCT," in Chapter 8. The program simply reads the file until it comes to the first blank record and uses it.

The method used here in the inventory example makes use of the first record in the file as an *end-of-file* indicator. Each time an entry is made in the file, and a file number (or disk address) is assigned by the program, that information is written in the first record. The date entered by the operator at the beginning of the business day is stored within the same record; thus, whenever an entry is made, the program can read the first record to "learn" the date and the present end-of-life address. The next entry, therefore, can be dated and placed in the next empty file space by the program. That address, in turn, is written back as the *new* end-of-file. Fig. 6–1 is a schematic representation of the file structure showing how the date and last file address are physically related to the disk file at sector 1. "Real" records begin with record numbers 1, 2, and 3 being assigned to sector 2, and succeeding groups of three subrecords being assigned in a similar manner to subsequent sectors.

After the program has determined and assigned the file number, or address, the operator is permitted to make the actual entry. The date, of course, has already been determined by the program without the operator's assistance. The operator will be prompted, in the following order, to enter the information for each field: class code, stock number

Program Listing 6–1. "INVENTORY"

PROGRAM INTRODUCTION

```
1000 CLEAR 250: REM INVENTORY, MBASIC VERS. 4.3
1010 ZZ$="B:STOCK.INV":GOSUB 1970
1020 D3=CVS(D$):LR=CVS(R$):CS$=CHR$(12):PRINT CS$
1030 PRINT"FILE HAS ";LR;" ENTRIES - DATED ";
1040 PRINT USING"##.##";D3
1050 PRINT"ENTER DATE AS (MM.DD) OR 0 TO SKIP";:INPUT D1
1060 IF D1=0 THEN 1100:REM DATE OK
1070 D3=D1:D4=INT(D3):D5=D3-D4:D6=100*D5+.1
1080 IF D4<1 OR D4>12 THEN 1050
1090 IF INT(D6)<1 OR INT(D6)>31 THEN 1050
1100 LSET D$=MKS$(D3):LSET    R$=MKS$(LR):PUT#2,1:CLOSE
1110 PRINT CS$
1120 PRINT"CHOOSE NEXT ACTIVITY":PRINT
1130 PRINT 1".ADD A NEW ITEM";TAB(35);2".CHANGE OR DELETE"
1140 PRINT 3".LIST ENTIRE STOCK";TAB(35);4".ITEMS ON ORDER"
1150 PRINT 5".FIND BY I.D.#",TAB(35);6".LIST LOW STOCK"
1160 PRINT 7".FIND BY FILE #";TAB(35);8".LIST BY CLASS-CODE"
1170 PRINT
1180 PRINT"SELECT";:INPUT Q:IF Q<1 OR Q>8 THEN 1180
1190 PRINT CS$:IF Q=>3 THEN 1670
```

MODIFICATIONS

```
1200 GOSUB 1970
1210 LR =CVS(R$):PRINT CS$:IF Q=1 THEN 1340
1220 PRINT:PRINT"FILE # TO CHANGE ";:INPUT F:GOSUB 2050
1230 GET#2,INT(X):GOSUB 1990
1240 GOSUB 2020:REM DECODE NUMBERS
1250 GOSUB 1940:LPRINT:REM PRINT IT
1260 PRINT"DELETE=1  NEW PRICE=2  MAJOR CHANGE=3  ESCAPE=4";
1270 INPUT Q:IF Q<>INT(Q) OR Q<1 OR Q>4 THEN 1260
1280 ON Q GOTO 1290,1320,1350,1110
1290 M=0:GOSUB 2010
1300 LSET N$=MKS$(N)
1310 GOTO 1610
1320 PRINT"NEW PRICE";:INPUT C:IF C>9999.99 THEN 1320
1330 LSET C$=MKS$(C):GOTO 1610
1340 PRINT"NEW ENTRY,FILE # WILL BE ";LR+1:PRINT
```

NEW AND MODIFIED ENTRIES

```
1350 PRINT "TYPE 'C' TO CONTINUE,'Q' TO QUIT";:INPUT Q$
1360 IF Q$<>"C" THEN CLOSE:GOTO 1110
1370 IF Q=1 THEN F=LR+1
1380 GOSUB 2050
1390 PRINT CS$:GOSUB 1990
1400 PRINT"CLASS CODE OR PREFIX";TAB(35);":";:INPUT Q$
1410 LSET CC$=LEFT$(Q$,2)
1420 PRINT"STOCK I.D ";TAB(35);":";:INPUT Q$
1430 LSET I$=LEFT$(Q$,12)
1440 PRINT"QUANTITY ON HAND";TAB(35);":";:INPUT QT
1450 PRINT"MINIMUM LEVEL";TAB(35);":";:INPUT M
1460 PRINT"QTY ON ORDER NOW";TAB(35);":";:INPUT O
1470 IF QT>99 OR M>99 OR O>99 THEN PRINT"MAX=99":GOTO 1440
1480 GOSUB 2010
1490 LSET N$=MKS$(N)
1500 PRINT"UNITS (EA,GR,DZ, ETC)";TAB(35);":";:INPUT Q$
1510 LSET U$=LEFT$(Q$,2)
1520 PRINT"COST PER UNIT/MSR";TAB(35);":";:INPUT C
1530 LSET C$=MKS$(C)
1540 PRINT"SHORT FORM DESCRIPT.";TAB(35);":";:INPUT Q$
1550 LSET DS$=LEFT$(Q$,14):PRINT"SPECIAL (Y/N) ";
1560 INPUT Q$:IF Q$="Y" THEN S$="**":GOTO 1580
1570 S$=""
1580 PRINT:PRINT"WRITE TO FILE (Y/N)";:INPUT Q$
1590 IF Q$="N" THEN F=F-1:GOTO 1350
1600 LSET D$=MKS$(D3):PRINT CS$
1610 PUT#2,INT(X):GOSUB 2020
1620 GOSUB 1940
1630 IF Q=2 THEN 1660
1640 GOSUB 1980
1650 LSET R$=MKS$(F):PUT#2,1
1660 PRINT CS$:CLOSE:GOTO 1110
```

Program Listing 6–1 (cont)

READ AND PRINT

```
1670 GOSUB 1970:REM DETERMINE END OF FILE   *
1680 LR=CVS(R$):Q$="" :IF Q<>7 THEN 1720
1690 PRINT"FILE NUMBER ";:INPUT F
1700 IF F<1 OR F>LR OR F<>INT(F) THEN 1690
1710 GOTO 2190
1720 IF Q=5 OR Q=8 THEN PRINT"CODE OR I.D.";:INPUT Q$
1730 LPRINT"STOCK AS OF ";:LPRINT USING"##.##";D3;
1740 RESTORE:GOSUB 2260
1750 LPRINT" "; SH$;" ";Q$
1760 LPRINT"FILE-DATE  ORD-MIN-QTY   CODE-NUMBER
1770 LPRINT"DESCRIPTION        PRICE     TOTAL"
1780 REM
1790 B=0
1800 FOR J=1 TO LR:S$="    ":FL=0
1810     F=J:GOSUB 2050
1820     GET#2,INT(X):GOSUB 1990
1830     B$="TOTAL VALUE=$#,#######.##":GOSUB 2020
1840     ON Q-2 GOSUB 2100,2120,2140,2170,2190,2240
1850     IF FL=0 THEN 1910
1860     IF M<1 THEN LPRINT USING"####";F;
1870     IF M<1 THEN LPRINT"=DELETED RECORD"
1880     IF M<1 THEN 1910
1890     GOSUB 1940
1900     B=B+(QT*C)
1910 NEXT J
1920 LPRINT:LPRINT USING B$;B:CLOSE:GOTO 1110
1930 REM SUBROUTINES TO FIELD AND PRINT   ********
1940 L$="#### ##.## ### ### ### \\ \\ \          \ "
1950 L1$="\                \ ###.## #####.##\\":L$=L$+L1$
1960 LPRINT USING L$;F,D,O,M,QT,U$,CC$,I$,DS$,C,C*QT,S$:RETURN
```

FILE HANDLING

```
1970 S=.333333: OPEN"R",2,ZZ$:GET#2,1
1980 FIELD#2,4 AS R$,4 AS D$,120 AS DY$:RETURN
1990 REM CALCULATE AND FIELD #2 FILE BUFFER **
2000 FIELD#2, Z*1 AS DY$,4 AS N$,4 AS D$,2 AS U$,4 AS C$,
     10 AS I$,14 AS DS$,2 AS CC$,2 AS S$:RETURN
2010 N=100*QT:N=100*(N+M):N=N+O:RETURN
2020 N=CVS(N$):C=CVS(C$):D=CVS(D$)
2030 QT=INT(N/10000):M=INT((N-10000*QT)/100)
2040 O=N-10000*QT-100*M:RETURN
2050 X=F*S+2.1-S:IF X-INT(X)<.2 THEN Z=0:RETURN
2060 IF X-INT(X)>.9 THEN Z=0:RETURN
2070 IF X-INT(X)<.5 THEN Z=42:RETURN
2080 IF X-INT(X)>.5 THEN Z=84:RETURN
```

Program Listing 6-1 (cont)

COMPARISON SUBROUTINES

```
2090 REM FIELD MATCHING ROUTINES***
2100 REM
2110 FL=1:RETURN:REM IF FL=1 THEN PRINT
2120 IF O>0 THEN FL=1
2130 RETURN
2140 I$=LEFT$(I$,LEN(Q$))
2150 IF I$=Q$ THEN FL=1
2160 RETURN
2170 IF QT<M THEN FL=1
2180 RETURN
2190 GOSUB 2050
2200 GET#2,INT(X):GOSUB 1990
2210 GOSUB 2020
2220 GOSUB 1940
2230 CLOSE:GOTO 1110
2240 IF CC$=Q$ THEN FL=1
2250 RETURN
2260 DATA"ALL ITEMS","ON ORDER","BY ID#","BY LOW STOCK"
2270 DATA"FILE#","CLASS-CODE"
2280 FOR XX9=3 TO Q:READ SH$:NEXT XX9
2290 RETURN
2300 CLOSE:GOTO 1120
```

or other unique identification, quantity on hand, minimum level, and number on order, followed by unit of measure, cost, description, and whether "special."

The method of handling the three quantities will bear some scrutiny. The numbers are "trapped" so that none of the three values can exceed 99. The justification for this is that the three numbers will be "packed" into one variable to save space, as seen in line 2020. The packing technique involves multiplying the quantity on hand by 100, and adding

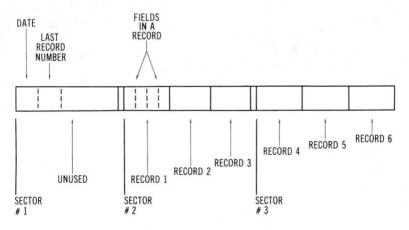

Fig. 6-1. Inventory file structure.

the minimum field to it. This new quantity is then multiplied by 100 and the number on order added to that figure. If all fields equaled 99, the resulting "packed" number would be 999999. This is the largest number that this version of BASIC can accommodate without going to "double-precision" form, which occupies twice as much file space per number. "Unpacking" is just the reverse of the pack function.

Corrections

Making corrections is essentially the same as making original entries. The operator provides the file number, which can be evaluated by the program as the disk address. The operator inputs the file number of the record to be changed. The program then locates the entry and prints it. By furnishing the correct response to "prompts," or messages appearing on the screen, the operator modifies the record's fields as necessary. The new version of the record is then written back in the file where it was before alteration. No other entries are affected. After modification, the new values are printed so that the operator may verify that the new values are correct.

Three kinds of changes are permitted: (1) price change, (2) deletion of the record in its entirety, and (3) a change of all fields. A deleted record remains in the file, but the message, "DELETED RECORD," will be printed whenever that file number is accessed by any except the modification option. The program deletes a record by simply entering a zero quantity in the field for minimum level; the remainder of the record is still there and the item can be reopened again by calling the modification routine and entering a number greater than zero for the "minimum" field. Changing the price requires only the entering of the new price. The choice of altering fields other than price is essentially the same as making a new entry, except that the record is written back to its original disk location and the end-of-file indicator is not updated.

Searching by Field

Up to this point, we have been considering the inventory as merely a list that may be occasionally updated. This has some utility, of course, as it can provide a neatly printed list for the operator's inspection or use. From this point on, the real value of an inventory program will be emphasized—the ability to locate an item, or items, by the use of any of several different criteria.

Although the example program is not an elaborate one, it permits finding and printing records in a number of different ways, as follows:

1. Direct access by the file number, which is evaluated as the disk address. This kind of search is nearly instantaneous and should be used whenever the file address is known. It may be known by looking at a previous listing.

2. Access by part number, serial number, or some other identifier that is unique to the particular item.
3. Find and list all items below the desired minimum level. This report tells the user which merchandise should be reordered.
4. Find and list all items presently on order.
5. Find and list all items having a common classification that has been previously established by the user. The classification might be a code for the manufacturer or a code for a broad type of material, such as motors, vacuum tubes, or canned vegetables.
6. Make a complete printout of everything that is in the inventory file.

All of the searches keep a running total of each item's value (unit cost times quantity on hand), which is printed as an aid to managing the financial problems associated with inventories. Fig. 6–2 shows the result of searching a small inventory by several methods. The entire list is printed first, for your reference, followed by the printed result of asking for a match with several different parameters.

PROGRAM ANALYSIS

The inventory program is shown in Program Listing 6–1. Figs. 6–3 and 6–4 are the system diagram and flowchart of the inventory system and program.

Program lines 1000–1190, when they are run, introduce the operator to the program. This section accomplishes several things that are more or less standard in business software. The opening section of any program should always define any key variables or arrays that might be used, name the file or files that will be accessed, and perform any other "housekeeping" functions that may be necessary. This portion of the example program reads the last date that was entered and allows the operator to either verify it or change it. It notifies the operator of the current file length; that is, how many entries already exist. It prints the "menu," which permits the operator to choose the activity he or she wishes to perform. Example 6–4 is a facsimile of the menu as it appears on the video screen.

Example 6–4. The Inventory "Menu"

```
FILE HAS 234 ENTRIES—DATED 10.30
ENTER DATE AS MM.DD OR 0 TO SKIP

CHOOSE NEXT ACTIVITY

1. ADD A NEW ITEM          2. CHANGE OR DELETE
3. LIST ENTIRE STOCK       4. ITEMS ON ORDER
5. FIND BY I.D. #          6. LIST LOW STOCK
7. FIND BY FILE #          8. LIST BY CLASS-CODE
```

STOCK AS OF 1.24 ALL ITEMS

FILE-DATE	ORD-MIN-QTY		CODE-NUMBER	DESCRIPTION	PRICE	TOTAL
1 1.24	0 3	2 EA 48	12345	TRANSISTOR	0.79	1.58
2 1.24	6 3	4 DZ 48	23998	RECTIFIER	1.25	5.00
3 1.24	4 4	1 EA MX	90000	MISSILE	625.00	625.00
4 1.24	0 12	12 GR MO	78-789	ELEC MOTOR	18.00	216.00

TOTAL VALUE=$ 847.58

STOCK AS OF 1.24 ON ORDER

FILE-DATE	ORD-MIN-QTY		CODE-NUMBER	DESCRIPTION	PRICE	TOTAL
2 1.24	6 3	4 DZ 48	23998	RECTIFIER	1.25	5.00
3 1.24	4 4	1 EA MX	90000	MISSILE	625.00	625.00

TOTAL VALUE=$ 630.00

STOCK AS OF 1.24 BY LOW STOCK

FILE-DATE	ORD-MIN-QTY		CODE-NUMBER	DESCRIPTION	PRICE	TOTAL
1 1.24	0 3	2 EA 48	12345	TRANSISTOR	0.79	1.58
3 1.24	4 4	1 EA MX	90000	MISSILE	625.00	625.00

TOTAL VALUE=$ 626.58

STOCK AS OF 1.24 CLASS-CODE 48

FILE-DATE	ORD-MIN-QTY		CODE-NUMBER	DESCRIPTION	PRICE	TOTAL
1 1.24	0 3	2 EA 48	12345	TRANSISTOR	0.79	1.58
2 1.24	6 3	4 DZ 48	23998	RECTIFIER	1.25	5.00

TOTAL VALUE=$ 6.58

STOCK AS OF 1.24 BY ID# 78-789

FILE-DATE	ORD-MIN-QTY		CODE-NUMBER	DESCRIPTION	PRICE	TOTAL
4 1.24	0 12	12 GR MO	78-789	ELEC MOTOR	18.00	216.00

TOTAL VALUE=$ 216.00

Fig. 6–2. Inventory printouts by search type.

Lines 1200–1660 perform the "add" and "change" functions, which differ in two major characteristics. Before the "change" function can be performed, the program has to know the file number to access, read it, and display it. And while the end-of-file indicator is updated for each new entry, it remains unchanged when an entry is merely modified.

Another major module of the program is found at lines 1670–1960. This section reads the file and prints the desired records. Special attention should be paid to how the desired records are identified and selected for printing. The reading takes place within the loop at line 1800; the reading begins at record number 1 and continues until "LR," which is the variable representing the end-of-file. All that remains is to sift the desired records out of the file for printing.

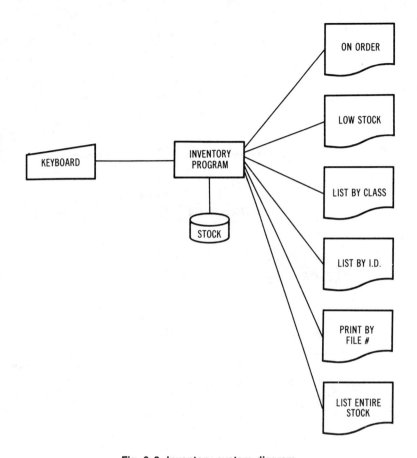

Fig. 6–3. Inventory system diagram.

Within the loop, there is a statement that uses the value of a variable, Q, which was established when the operator chose the menu option to be used. The value of Q determines which of six subroutines will be accessed for comparison. These subroutines will be found at line 2100 onward. The subroutine at line 2170 will serve as an example. It says that if QT (quantity on hand) is less than M (minimum stock level), the flag variable, FL, will be set equal to 1. The program flow returns to the loop, the remainder of which has been conditioned to PRINT if FL = 1 and skip if it is zero. The result of this kind of search, and others, can be seen in the sample printouts, Fig. 6–2.

The other subroutines associated with the read-and-print loop work in a similar way. The selected field in each record is compared with the chosen parameter and either printed or skipped as a result of the

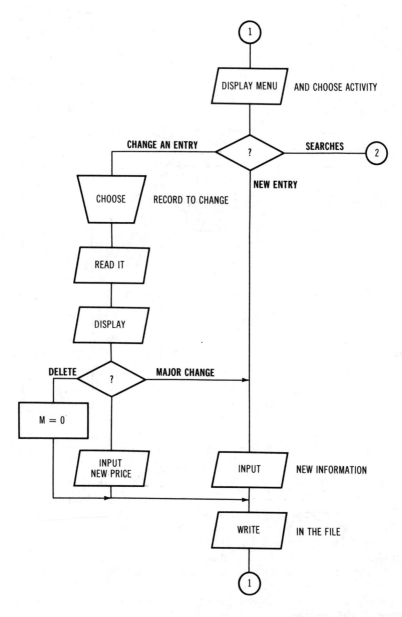

Fig. 6–4. Flowchart of the

evaluation. This loop, therefore, makes two separate decisions for the program. It decides which subroutine to use for evaluation of the record, and then decides whether to accept (and print) or reject the record it has just read.

The remaining program lines, not included in the previous descriptions of program functions, deal with "housekeeping" chores such as finding the disk address and coding and decoding the records. Some of these functions are unique to the family of BASICs this one is a part of, and have no direct equivalent in other languages.

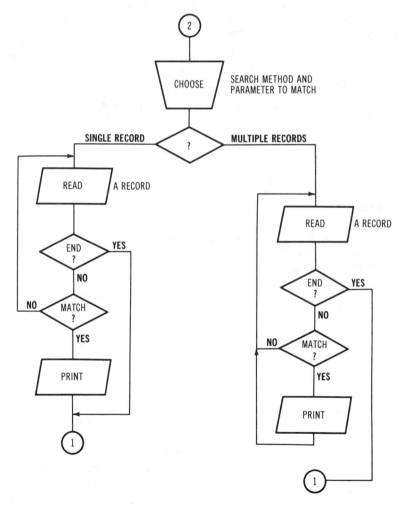

program, "INVENTORY."

PROGRAM EVALUATION

The example program will now be evaluated with regard to its usefulness and its faults. The primary criteria for evaluating any inventory system are its *storage capacity* and its *speed of retrieval*. The reader desiring to purchase an inventory software package, rather than write one, may find the following paragraphs a guide to evaluating a prospective purchase.

Storage Capacity

In any computer inventory, the storage capacity is a function of *record length* and *disk space,* and there is a trade-off between these two features even in the largest systems.

First, consider the minidiskettes described in an earlier chapter. The 5-inch size, in its single-density configuration, can hold no more than 90,000 bytes. Simple calculation reveals that this space represents 900 records of 100 bytes each. In practice, the maximum is seldom achieved because 100% effective use of space is difficult. In the example program, the BASIC that is used confines us to 128 byte sectors, which we divide into three subrecords, with a resultant loss of two bytes per sector. And in similar hardware systems, where soft sectoring uses some of the available space, there is additional wastage. Certain other computer systems avoid some types of loss but reserve space for other functions, such as directories of the disk contents, and as a result few, if any, systems effectively use the entire surface of the disk.

There are, of course, greater densities of format and larger diskettes. Nevertheless, the small-system inventory will always have some upper limit in size, which can be increased only by adding disk space or reducing record size. Presently available small-business software packages hold from 1000 to several thousand entries. The example program uses 42-byte records and, depending on the operating system that is used, can effectively manage 1200 to 1800 of these relatively short records on one 5-inch, single-density disk.

Speed of Access

The second important criterion of evaluation is *speed of retrieval*. Direct access by the file (address) number has been mentioned as being the most immediate means of accessing a record. There are other rapid means of access to be discussed a little later in the chapter, but the fact remains that some searches, at least, will require reading the entire file and testing each record for some desired parameter. For these operations, the time involved is a direct function of the file length and the mechanical speed of the disk system, and simply cannot be accelerated except by superior hardware that will operate faster. In practice, the hardship of slow speed becomes somewhat less of a limit because the printer is even slower.

Except in the largest systems, where memory space is not very limited, the inventory will be able to retrieve rapidly on only one or two key fields. (Memory permitting, arrays containing several fields, representing several kinds of search, can be established and searched much more rapidly than is the case when dealing with the disk file itself. This technique is seldom applied to small machines due to the memory requirement.)

One possibility, besides the file address, is to use the unique *serial* or *part number*. If this form of addressing is implemented, the program must use either a sorted file or an algorithm such as the "hash" method described elsewhere. In most instances, in the small-business category, the user must be prepared to wait several minutes for an extended search-and-print operation to be completed.

RAPID SEARCH METHODS

It was mentioned briefly in Chapter 5 that some rather refined methods of addressing file records exist, and that they are worthwhile for large data bases. Inventory is the ideal type of problem for experimenting with these methods. Where every record in a file must be read, in order to find the right one (an unsorted file, obviously), the search time can run to several minutes. This is a long time in computer terms. It can be shortened to seconds by using a sorted file, or one of the more mathematical search methods. These techniques are not economical or recommended for files involving fewer than 1000 records.

Explanations of sorting and searching methods comprise entire volumes. One of the best sources is by Donald Knuth.[1] Here are some brief examples:

Merging

A randomly organized file is divided into two or more shorter files. The first record of each is read and compared with the other(s). They are placed in correct order, and the next two (or more) likewise compared and exchanged. This procedure is repeated until in the end there is one file, properly organized.

Binary Search

A file already sorted is searched for a particular key. The program reads the middle key; that is, in a file 1000 items long, the 500th key is read. Unless you get lucky and hit the desired key the first time, it will be found in either the upper or lower half of the list. The selected one-half is again divided in half, and again redivided until the key is matched. This may sound repetitious, but on the average any record in a 1000-item file can be found in less than 10 tries. This is a common technique in large-business software. It requires extra memory and file space, as well as a longer program. Unless thousands of items are to be handled, the small-machine software can dispense with such a feature.

Hashing

One of the most fascinating methods is referred to as *hashing*. In hashing, the proper file address is determined by the key field itself, using appropriate algorithms. The records are scattered about in the file as they are entered. The same algorithm looks for a desired record using the same technique. Although any address is not totally unique to a particular key, those with similar hash-determined addresses will at least be grouped in approximately the right place. Searches that would otherwise take minutes are reduced to seconds, a significant gain if large files are involved.

Again, the reader is advised to research the subject separately, as it is much too detailed to be found in a text of this size and at this level of programming.

SUMMARY

The inventory package used here for illustration uses one (rather long) program and one file. Larger inventory sets may have several programs and several files for different purposes, such as a temporary daily file into which daily changes are entered. This file is then used to update the main inventory at the end of the day. They may also have a means of sorting the file data to permit quicker location by a unique identifier, such as the manufacturer's part number. Small operations "make do" with only one program and one file. This means that the main file is accessed for every transaction of every kind. In such cases, the inventory is merely another kind of storage and retrieval, with a few extra features.

The extra features in this case are the ability to search by a variety of parameters—file number (the fastest means), stock number, class-code, items on order, and items below minimum level. The program also totals the value of items located by any search. By choosing to print the entire stock, the dollars-and-cents total value will be revealed. Such a list and total is valuable any time but is particularly worthwhile when closing books for accounting or tax purposes.

This program differs from most of the others used in the book by being written in one of the Microsoft family of BASICs, which are characterized by features some programmers find difficult to use. Among these are the rather complex file-handling instructions and the "rounding errors" mentioned briefly in Chapter 2. There are also some welcome advanced features involving the use of two-letter variables, improved string-handling, and logic functions. This BASIC will be often encountered, as versions of it appear on many of the more popular low-priced computers.

The program used in this chapter is sufficient for many small businesses. Its major drawback is that the file is not sorted and there is no particularly fast way to locate any item, or items, except by file number. It is adequate if only a thousand or so entries are needed, and if speed is not of major importance. Most of the remarks that normally document a program had to be removed in an attempt to minimize program length. This detracts from its readability but not from its usefulness. It is thus our "exception to the rule" about internal documentation.

It also provides an interesting contrast with the remainder of this book's programs, most of which were written in another BASIC (North Star). A comparison by the reader will reveal several differences in style, structure, and documentation.

In summary, an inventory program, program set, or package is simply a list stored within the facility of a computer, and the means by which it can be viewed and/or modified. Each item of the list, or record, contains several fields. Each field contains a specific type of information; that is, the part number, the quantity on hand, and so forth. An inventory differs from any other list in that a record can be identified by, and retrieved by, any of the several fields. This permits close monitoring and control of the stock.

One of the most significant limiting factors of any inventory program is the number of records it can accommodate. This is as much a function of the hardware as it is of the program; clever programming can condense it a bit, but generally speaking there is a limit to the space on even large disks. The small 5-inch single-density floppy is good for between one and two thousand records per diskette, depending on the record size and the operating system. Larger, more-dense formats offer proportionately greater capacity.

Another common deficiency is having too few fields to handle all the information the user needs. This points up the compromise needed between record size and records per disk.

Last, but not least, is the speed of retrieval. By their nature, inventory records will be difficult, if not impossible, to keep sorted in any consistent manner. If maximum speed is desired, the program must incorporate some rather precise and rapid means of locating the item in the file, usually by a part number.

In designing an inventory, or evaluating one, look for the following features. Not all qualities are indispensable or to be found in more modest programs; however, they *are* a standard of comparison.

- Number of records allowable. Will that meet your present needs, with a suitable margin for expansion?
- Speed of search. This becomes more important as the number of items increases. Is speed worth what it costs in terms of expense, program length, and memory requirements?

- Number of fields per record. Are there unnecessary fields, which for your use only waste disk space?
- Do you need some features that are not provided? (A field to compute turns per year, for example.) This just might outweigh all other advantages.

SELF-HELP TEST QUESTIONS

1. What is an inventory?
2. Name some of the "fields" an inventory list contains.
3. Which field is the main identifier for the item?
4. How can the total value of stock be found?
5. How can a computer inventory help the business?

REFERENCE

1. Knuth, D.E. *The Art of Computer Programming. Volume 3: Sorting and Searching.* Addison-Wesley Publishing Co., Inc., Reading, MA, 1973.

7

Payroll Programs

OBJECTIVES

This chapter describes the following:

- What makes up a payroll system, whether it is a manual one or one that is computerized.
- How a computer prints a check or other prepared form.
- A typical small-business payroll set, with provision for storing employee data and calculating taxes and pay.
- What to include in payroll files, and how to do so.

Payroll accounting is undoubtedly one of the most complex functions for which the small business will ever use its computer. It is probably the last business activity that should be computerized, as it is more subject to error than the accounting functions in Chapter 8, and more complex in structure than an inventory system. Nevertheless, it is the first function many businesses want automated. Once implemented and debugged, a computer payroll can handle 1000 employees as easily as one, but somewhere between those extremes will be a point where it is still easier to do it by hand.

PAYROLL REQUIREMENTS

The requirements of a simple, practical payroll system are as follows:

1. Keep a *master file* of all employees. This will include for each, the person's name and address, social security number, employee number, and pay rate. It will record exemptions for tax purposes, overtime provisions, and any miscellaneous additions or subtractions from the individual's pay. With a few more items it could conceivably be the individual's complete history of employment with the company.

2. Maintain a *table of tax rates* which can be applied for various levels of income and combinations of tax exemptions. With a computer system, this might be a separate file or, if kept simple enough, it could be made an integral part of the program.
3. Provide sufficient storage space and details to enable monthly, quarterly, or annual reports to be generated. This information would include, for example, total year-to-date earnings and deductions.
4. Make all necessary calculations to determine the gross pay, deductions, and the employee's net paycheck figure.

Observe that these steps are equally necessary in either a manual or a computerized system. The more elaborate payroll programs are designed so that on each payday they print a summary of pay details for everyone and, in some cases, the paychecks themselves. These more elaborate programs will also keep the check register and perhaps charge each worker's pay to specific jobs, or projects, as a form of cost analysis. Such features can be valuable to larger firms.

Probably yearly, the programmer will have to alter the *tax tables* to conform with new laws. If there are other than state and federal taxes to be calculated, or if there are union checkoffs or other mandatory deductions, these deduction steps will have to be added to any except the most elaborate "canned" payrolls. With so many variables and possible exceptions it is almost a certainty that any computerized payroll system will be riddled with errors and bugs until it has been in use for some time. It is advisable for the business to continue with their previous manual payroll methods for several pay periods after acquiring a computer, in order to verify the accuracy of the payroll program.

PRINTING ON PREPARED FORMS

Persons acquiring a computerized payroll system for the first time are usually intrigued by the idea of having a computer program print the checks. Programming for this is not difficult, and the same applies to printing on invoices or other forms. It is only necesssary to lay out blank paper in the image of the form and rearrange a group of "PRINT" statements until the spacing between items is exactly right. It is also necessary to procure the checks in a continuously rolled or folded form that will work with the printer. Once this form of preparing checks or other documents has been established, it may be difficult to switch back to manual methods and "unmodify" the affected programs. A good supply of forms and checks, therefore, should be kept on hand once this kind of operation has been initiated.

Two realities work against this scheme. First of all, when configured for the computer's printer, the business forms themselves are usually more expensive than the standard type that they have replaced. Second, it is a nuisance to remove the paper from the printer, load the preprinted forms, align them exactly, and then reverse the process to get back to normal printing. The cost effectiveness approaches zero unless a great many checks are to be printed at one time, or unless a separate printer can be kept loaded with check forms at all times. If this feature is required, the user can order the necessary forms and checks from one of the many companies that specialize in business forms for computer use. They may be listed in the yellow pages of your telephone book, or you may be able to learn of suitable sources from your bank or from any computer company in your area. To order the forms, you will have to specify the printer that will be used, and the program will have to be modified to fit the form.

PROGRAM DEVELOPMENT

We will divide the development of a fairly simple payroll package into the following functions:

1. Create and maintain the *master employee data file*.
2. Enter the time-card information at payday time.
3. Make all the necessary calculations.
4. Print the *payday report*.

Fig. 7-1 is the diagram of a payroll system that can be used to accomplish these goals. As we are dealing with small businesses

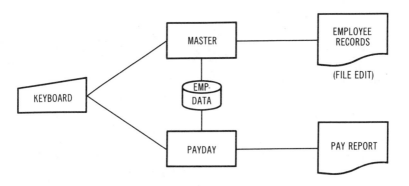

Fig. 7–1. Payroll system diagram.

throughout this book, the function of check writing and periodic reporting can be left to the bookkeeper or accountant. This will keep the program simple enough to understand and small enough to run in a small machine.

83

This small, relatively simple package will have the following programs and files:

Programs

MASTER	(Enter and edit the employee data.)
PAYDAY	(Enter hours, etc., on payday, calculate pay, and print listing.)

Files

EMPDATA   (Employee data and historical records.)

For purposes of illustration, we will try to get by with two programs (MASTER and PAYDAY) and one data file (EMPDATA). The package will generate two printed reports, as noted in Fig. 7-1. These are the so-called *file edit* (a printout of the entire file for inspection or verification) and the *pay report* that is generated at pay time. The first report contains the information pertinent to the employees, such as their social security number, their exemptions, and so on, and a record of year-to-date earnings and deductions. This report can be printed at any time that it may be needed. The payday report, on the other hand, is produced only when the program is being "run" to calculate current pay and deductions. Both reports, at such time as they may be generated, will contain the latest year-to-date totals for all earnings, taxes, and net pay. These totals become a part of each individual employee's record in the master file. So that a separate file of tax rates will not be needed, *tax tables* will be made a part of the program, "PAYDAY." These simplifications will permit us to accomplish the most important payroll functions with only one file and two programs.

It should be noted here that this is really a very minimal payroll system, suitable for small businesses with from ten to several tens of employees. Smaller businesses cannot benefit from even a small computerized payroll, and much larger businesses may want something more sophisticated. This package works, but it is used here mainly as an example. A really good payroll package may have 20 or 30 programs and files, and may be able to print a multitude of different reports. More important to the small business, it may require more memory, larger disks, and generally more expensive equipment than the business is prepared to buy for the purpose. Payrolls are generally considered to be the most complex and difficult of business software.

THE MASTER FILE

Creating the master file should be familiar by now as a fairly straightforward information storage and retrieval exercise. The only difference between it and previous examples is the makeup of the record fields. Fields typical in larger payroll programs are listed as follows:

- Name 1 (last name).
- Name 2 (first and middle).
- Address 1 (street or box number).
- Address 2 (city and state).
- Address 3 (zip code).
- Social security number.
- Pay classification.
- Salary, if applicable.
- Hourly rate, if applicable.
- Overtime rate, if applicable.
- Number of tax exemptions.
- Yearly and quarterly pay history.
- All deductions such as dues, insurance, etc.

This is more detail than a simple payroll program need support; it can be stripped to its essentials for our purposes. A record such as listed might take as many as 200 bytes of storage space on a disk, depending on how much detail is needed in each field. On a small system, storage space is at a premium so the records should be kept as small as possible. In actual fact, the records in our sample program have been made 100 bytes in length, which is adequate and even leaves some "spare" space for additions that might become necessary.

Elaborate payrolls provide space for payroll savings, insurance contributions, union dues, and so forth. The complications are sometimes avoided by simply providing fields for "deductions" 1 through 9 with their function being assigned independently by the user. We will include two such fields in the demonstration program; they will be numbered 1 and 2. If they are not used, the operator simply enters zero in those fields when entering payroll data.

Sorting by last name has been mentioned in previous chapters. Some programs provide for doing this at pay time, while others allow the master file to be resorted into alphabetical, last-name order each time a new name is added. For companies with less than a few dozen employees, this is probably an unnecessary luxury that merely consumes program space. If the operation is widespread, it may be desirable to sort addresses (mainly the zip code) to enable consolidated mailings of checks to other offices. This usually does not concern the really small business.

The reader desiring to sort employee records by last name, for any purpose, should review Chapter 5. The name and address program used there as an illustration of sort methods can be easily modified to become a payroll employee file program. It is only necessary to provide for the additional information fields in each record.

MASTER PAYROLL PROGRAM

The program, "MASTER," is essentially a rerun of storage and retrieval programs as described in previous chapters. It must provide for making the original entries and for changing them from time to time, adding or removing employees, or changing their rate of pay or their deductions. Although sorting the file occasionally to get everyone back in alphabetical order is a handy feature, it is not indispensable.

This program (and its associated file, "EMPDATA") will handle all the information about the employees necessary to pay them and keep a running record of the year-to-date figures for gross pay, taxes, deductions, and net pay.

Fig. 7-2 is the flow diagram of "MASTER," the file maintenance program. Notice the similarity in the use of "MASTER" and "EMPDATA" to the previous storage/retrieval programs.

The "MASTER" software is provided in Program Listing 7-1. Example 7-1 is a sample *employee history* display as it appears on the video screen. This can be viewed at any time for review purposes by choosing the "EMPLOYEE HISTORY" option from the menu and typing in the number of the employee whose record you wish to examine.

Example 7-1. Employee History Display

EMPLOYEE NBR 2	YEAR TO DATE:	6. GROSS PAY	437.50
1. SUZY SALESPERSON		7. FEDERAL W.T.	40.84
2. SS #987-65-4321		* STATE W.T.	18.62
3. STATUS (M OR S)	S	* FICA WITHHELD	26.82
4. DEDUCTIONS	1	8. OTHER-1	4.50
5. SALARY	125.00	* OTHER-2	13.00
* HOURLY	.00	9. NET PAY	334.12
* O.T. RATE	.00		
		99. WRITE TO FILE	

SELECT NBR TO CHANGE, 0 FOR NO CHANGE

This option is first used to enter information about a new employee and may be used at a later date when there has been a change in the employee's status, such as pay rate or tax exemptions. With the exception of these uses, this option will seldom be used. Changes are made, when required, by simply selecting the number of the field to be changed and entering the new information.

ENTERING EMPLOYEE DATA

At such time as the payroll program is first implemented, the basic information about each employee must be entered as just described, by

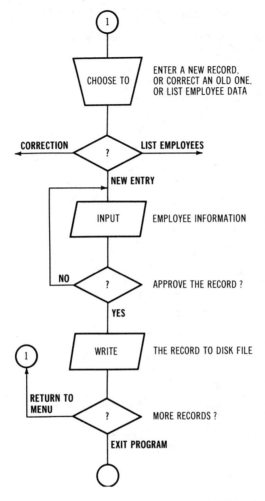

Fig. 7–2. Flowchart of the program, "MASTER."

use of the "EMPLOYEE HISTORY" option. The information will be that which identifies the employee, his or her rate of pay, and his or her tax status. As the payroll will likely not be started at exactly the first of the year, year-to-date earnings and deductions will have to be provided to the record by the operator. After this has been done once, the program takes care of updating the earnings information on future paydays.

The file for an individual employee, or all employees, can be inspected at any time and changed if necessary. Except for occasional

Program Listing 7-1. "MASTER"

```
1000 REM PROGRAM MASTER (PAYROLL) NORTH STAR REL.4
1010 DIM N$(20),S$(11),M$(1)
1020 L=10\REM CHANGE L FOR NUMBER OF RECORDS
1030 REM FILES OF DIFFERENT LENGTH
1040 PRINT CHR$(12)\REM CLEAR SCREEN CHARACTER
1050 PRINT"EMPLOYEE MASTER FILE"\FOR X=1 TO 20
1060 PRINT"*",\NEXT X\PRINT"*"\PRINT
1065 PRINT"0. EXIT PROGRAM"
1070 PRINT"1. EMPLOYEE HISTORY"
1080 PRINT"2. YEAR TO DATE RECORDS"
1090 PRINT"3. DELETE AN EMPLOYEE"
1100 PRINT"4. CREATE NEW FILE"\PRINT
1110 PRINT"SELECT",\INPUT A\IF A=0 THEN CHAIN"PAYMENU"
1120 IF A<1 OR A>4 OR A<>INT(A) THEN 1110
1130 ON A GOTO 1150,1640,2220,2010
1140 REM
1150 PRINT"ENTER EMPLOYEE NUMBER, 1 TO ",L,\INPUT Q
1155 IF Q<1 THEN 1150
1160 IF Q<1 OR Q>L  OR Q<>INT(Q) THEN 1150
1170 PRINT\PRINT\OPEN#1,"EMPDATA"
1180 GOSUB 1800\REM TO READ THE RECORD
1190 IF E=-1 THEN PRINT"NO RECORD FOR",Q
1200 PRINT\PRINT
1210 IF E>0 THEN 1330
1220 PRINT"NEW EMPLOYEE (Y/N)",\INPUT Q$
1230 IF Q$="N" THEN CLOSE#1\IF Q$="N" THEN 1040
1240 REM
1250 REM FIND BLANK RECORD
1260 FOR X=1 TO L\Q=X
1270      GOSUB 1800
1280      IF E>0 THEN 1300
1290      IF E<0 THEN EXIT 1310
1300 NEXT X
1310 GOSUB 2200
1320 E=X\Q=X\N$="EMPLOYEE NAME"
1330 GOSUB 1830
1340 PRINT\INPUT"SELECT NBR TO CHANGE, 0 FOR NO CHANGE ",Q
1350 IF Q=99 THEN 1990\IF Q=0 THEN CLOSE#1\IF Q=0 THEN 1040
1360 IF Q<1 OR Q>14 OR Q<>INT(Q) THEN 1340
1370 ON Q GOTO 1380,1410,1440,1470,1500,1540,1550,1600,1620
1380 INPUT"NAME (20 CHAR)    :",N$
1390 IF LEN(N$)>20 THEN N$=N$(1,20)
1400 N$=" "+N$\GOTO 1330
1410 INPUT" S.S.#(NNNNNNNNN) ",S$
1420 IF LEN(S$)<>9 THEN 1410
1430 S$=S$(1,3)+"-"+S$(4,5)+"-"+S$(6,9)\GOTO 1330
1440 INPUT"MARITAL STATUS    :",M$
1450 IF M$="M" THEN 1470\IF M$="S" THEN 1470
1460 GOTO 1440
1470 INPUT"NUMBER DEDUCTIONS:",D
1480 IF D<0 OR D>10 THEN 1470\D=INT(D)
1490 GOTO 1330
1500 INPUT"WEEKLY SALARY ",S1
```

Program Listing 7–1 (cont)

```
1510 IF S1>0 THEN 1330
1520 INPUT"HOURLY RATE ",H
1530 INPUT"O.T. RATE ",O\GOTO 1330
1540 INPUT"GROSS PAY",G\GOTO 1330
1550 INPUT"Y.T.D. FEDERAL W.T.",F1
1560 IF F<0 OR F>10000 THEN 1550
1570 INPUT"STATE TAX",S2
1580 IF S2<0 OR S2>10000 THEN 1570
1590 INPUT"FICA TAX",F2\GOTO 1330
1600 INPUT"OTHER - 1 ",O1
1610 INPUT"OTHER - 2 ",O3\GOTO 1330
1620 INPUT"NET PAY ",N\GOTO 1330
1630 REM
1640 REM YEAR TO DATE PRINTOUT
1650 OPEN#1,"EMPDATA"
1660 FOR X=1 TO L\Q=X
1670         GOSUB 1800\REM READ FILE
1680         IF E<0 THEN 1700
1690         GOSUB 2050\REM PRINT IT
1700 NEXT X
1710 CLOSE#1\GOTO 1040
1720 REM READ AND DISPLAY EMPLOYEE
1730 OPEN#1,"EMPDATA"
1740 FOR X=1 TO L\Q=X
1750         GOSUB 1800\REM READ FILE
1760         IF E<0 THEN 1780
1770         GOSUB 1830\REM DISPLAY
1780 NEXT X
1790 CLOSE#1\GOTO 1040
1800 READ#1%Q*100,E\IF E<0 THEN RETURN
1810 READ#1%Q*100,E,N$,S$,M$,D,S1,H,O,G,F1,S2,F2,O1,O3,N
1820 RETURN
1830 PRINT\REM DISPLAY FOLLOWS
1840 PRINT"   EMPLOYEE NBR",E,TAB(20),"YEAR TO DATE:   ",
1850 PRINT"6. GROSS PAY   ",%9F2,G
1860 PRINT"1.",N$,TAB(35),"7. FEDERAL W.T.",%9F2,F1
1870 PRINT"2. SS #",S$,TAB(35),"*. STATE W.T.  ",%9F2,S2
1880 PRINT"3. STATUS (M or S)",TAB(19),M$,TAB(35),
1890 PRINT"*. FICA WITHHELD",%8F2,F2
1900 PRINT"4. DEDUCTIONS ",TAB(19),D,TAB(35),"8. OTHER-1",
1910 PRINT "   ",%10F2,O1
1920 PRINT"5. SALARY",TAB(15),%7F2,S1,TAB(35),"*. OTHER-2",
1930 PRINT TAB(50),%9F2,O3
1940 PRINT"*. HOURLY",TAB(15),%7F2,H, TAB(35),"9. NET PAY",
1950 PRINT TAB(50),%9F2,N
1960 PRINT"*. O.T. RATE",TAB(15),%7F2,O
1970 PRINT TAB(35),"99. WRITE TO FILE"
1980 RETURN
1990 WRITE#1%E*100,E,N$,S$,M$,D,S1,H,O,G,F1,S2,F2,O1,O3,N
2000 CLOSE#1\GOTO 1040
```

Program Listing 7–1 (cont)

```
2010 CREATE"EMPDATA",INT(L/2)\OPEN#1,"EMPDATA"
2020 FOR X=1 TO L
2030     WRITE#1%X*100,-1
2040 NEXT X\WRITE#1%0,1\CLOSE#1\GOTO 1040
2050 REM
2060 REM MASTER FILE EDIT
2070 PRINT#1,CHR$(10)\PRINT#1,E,TAB(5),N$,TAB(26),S$,
2080 PRINT#1,TAB(38),"SAL=",
2090 PRINT#1%6F2,S1,TAB(40),%6F2,H," PER.HR ",TAB(50),
2100 PRINT#1%7F2,O," O.T. RATE"\PRINT#1,"STATUS=",M$,"
2105 PRINT#1,D," DEDUCTIONS"
2110 PRINT#1,"YEAR-TO-DATE RECORD:",
2120 PRINT#1,TAB(22),"GROSS=",TAB(30),%10F2,G,
2130 PRINT#1,TAB(50),"OTHER-1",%12F2,O1
2140 PRINT#1,TAB(22),"FED TAX",TAB(30),%10F2,F1,
2150 PRINT#1,TAB(50),"OTHER-2",%12F2,O3
2160 PRINT#1,TAB(22),"ST. TAX",TAB(30),%10F2,S2,
2170 PRINT#1,TAB(50),"NET PAY",%12F2,N
2180 FOR Y=1 TO 5\PRINT#1,CHR$(10)\NEXT\REM BLANK LINES
2190 RETURN
2200 N$=" "\M$=" "\S$=" "\    D=0\S1=0\H=0\O=0\G=0
2210 F1=0\S2=0\F2=0\O1=0\O3=0\N=0\RETURN
2220 REM DELETION RTN
2225 INPUT"DELETE AN EMPLOYEE (Y/N) ",Q$
2226 IF Q$<>"Y" THEN 1040\OPEN#1,"EMPDATA"
2230 INPUT"EMPLOYEE NUMBER TO DELETE",Q
2240 GOSUB 1800\REM READ RECORD
2250 GOSUB 1830\REM DISPLAY IT
2260 INPUT"DELETE IT (Y/N) ",Q$
2270 IF Q$<>"Y" THEN CLOSE#1\IF Q$<>"Y"THEN 1040
2280 WRITE#1%Q*100,-1
2290 CLOSE#1\GOTO 1040
```

changes, the program, "MASTER," will be used very infrequently after being originally installed in the system. To summarize "MASTER":

1. Run "MASTER." Open file "EMPDATA."
2. Input the following information for first employee:
   a. Name.
   b. Social security number.
   c. Salary or rate of pay, if hourly.
   d. Married or single, and number of exemptions.
   e. Any other deductions.
3. If entry is correct, write it in the file.
4. Do the same for the next one, or close file and exit the program.
5. Whenever desired, run "MASTER" and view, or print, the employee's history.
6. If necessary, call the record and modify it.

As it is written, "MASTER" assigns the *payroll number* to each employee as his or her data are entered. The operator may ask for any number within the range of the program; if such an employee already exists, his or her record will be displayed. If not, the program will prompt with "NEW EMPLOYEE (Y/N)?" If the operator responds with Y (Yes), the program will assign the next "vacant" number to the new employee. If a range of numbers has been established as 1 to 10, as it has been in the sample program, requested numbers less than 1 or more than 10 will be rejected. If 6 was the last assigned number, and the operator asks for number 9, the program will ignore the 9 and assign number 7 to the new employee. If, in this same case, an employee number 2 has recently been deleted from the records, the program will assign that number to the new employee. In other words, the program chooses the lowest available blank record.

The maximum number of employees has been set to 10 at line 1020 of program "MASTER." To accommodate more employees, it is necessary to change the value of the variable, L, to *the number of records you feel will be necessary*.

If some other convention is to be used for "numbering" employees, a program modification is needed. The method used here has been adopted, as have many of this book's program features, to reduce the program to its simplest practical state, without destroying its usefulness.

Corrections or deletions follow a procedure similar to the original entries. It is necessary only to call for the pay number and enter the new data when prompted to do so.

PAYROLL ENTRIES AND CALCULATIONS

The next step assumes that the master file exists and that the hours have been turned in for the period. The work details will be entered by the operator who then runs the program that does the calculations, but first a word about the use of tables in computer programs.

Tables are in common use in computer programs for the same reason that they are used in any other activity. Anyone who has prepared an income-tax return is familiar with the tables that go with the short-form tax calculations. These tables are a list of income figures with, for each income listed, an amount of tax due. In addition to the tax due for that exact income (for example, $15,000 annually), there will be a percentage figure to be applied to all income greater than $15,000 and less than some higher amount (such as $18,000). This list is called a table. Although this is simpler, for the average person, than manipulating complicated algorithms, it nevertheless requires some attention.

There are two ways of incorporating tables (of any kind) into programs, and two different ways of using them. If the tables are complex, they may be stored in a data file and called when needed by the program. If they are brief, they may be made part of the program itself. The latter method is the simplest.

Once the program has access to the data, there are again two ways of using them. In one system, the program has a "key" that directly accesses the address of the particular data needed. Again, if the data is not extensive there is a simpler way to do it. The following program segment is in BASIC and uses statements that will work directly in nearly every version. It makes use of an IF-THEN statement which compares the gross salary with the IF argument. When they match, the THEN function makes the calculation. All nonapplicable rates will be skipped.

This is part of the information to calculate the Montana state tax for 1980. Previous to this part of the program, the gross pay has been calculated and *annualized;* that is, multiplied by 52 if it is a weekly payroll, or by 12 if it is a monthly payroll. The tax is then calculated on the basis of the equivalent annual income, which is how the tables are printed. After the annual tax is found at that rate of pay, the tax is divided by 52 (for weekly equivalent) or by 12 (for the monthly equivalent). This may result in some inequity if the employee's pay varies from pay period to pay period, but at the end of the year he or she can adjust it when filing the tax return.

Example 7-2. Sample State Tax Calculation

```
1470 REM BEGIN TAX TABLES
1480 REM FOR MONTANA TAX WHETHER SINGLE OR MARRIED
1490 IF G1> 35000 THEN S3 = (G1 − 35000)*.121 + 3135
1500 IF G1> 20000 AND G1< 35000 THEN
     S3 = (G1 − 20000)*.11 + 1485
```

Line 1500 is simply the expression, in BASIC, that corresponds to the tax bracket of $20,000 to $35,000 per year, after standard deductions have been taken. From eight to 10 additional lines would be required to enter the entire table (see Program Listing 7-2). This particular line says that if the employee earned between $20,000 and $35,000 annually, he owes $1485 plus 11% of all over $20,000.

When this short segment is augmented with lines for all the necessary tax rates, it yields the tax due with an accuracy no better, and no worse, than would the same tables used in the old-fashioned, "look-it-up" way. In this program, we have spaced the lines of the table in steps of several thousand dollars at the upper income end of the table. If this is not sufficient accuracy, the user can add program lines, as necessary, up to and including as many lines as there are in the source tables. Such accuracy is seldom required until the time the taxpayer is ready to file his final report. The main consideration is to keep the employee in the correct bracket, so that he or she will not end the year with a significant shortage or overpayment of withheld taxes.

Exactly the same method is used to calculate the federal tax, except that the federal tax tables "care" whether or not the employee is married; thus, twice as large a table is required. The FICA tax is found in the same manner; the exception with FICA is that it has to be deducted until the maximum amount has been collected, then discontinued for the rest of the year. This should be done by detecting, at the beginning of each series of FICA tax calculations, whether the maximum has already been paid. To learn how this is done, see lines 1830–1910 in Program Listing 7-2.

ENTERING PAY DATA

On payday, the operator calls for the employee records, one at a time, verifies that the basic information is correct, and inputs the hours worked. In the sample program, provision is made for paying weekly. This is satisfactory in most instances. Complex payrolls allow for paying weekly, monthly, or semimonthly. This vastly complicates the program. As the program is going to do most of the work, it is feasible to do the task each week regardless of the schedule on which the checks are actually delivered to the payee.

PAY PROCEDURE

The preceding paragraphs have prepared us for the actual running of the payroll, the reason for the existence of the entire package. Please refer to Program Listing 7-2 and the flowchart, Fig. 7-3. "PAYDAY" is another one of those business programs in which the date is important. In the opening lines, the operator is "prompted" to enter the current date and cannot proceed without doing so. The date entered should be the *effective date of the pay period* being used. The next request made by the program is for an employee number. When a number is typed in by the operator, a sequence of events is set in motion.

First, the program opens the master file and reads the entire record for the employee whose number was entered. If there is no valid employee by that number, an error message will be displayed and another number requested. The name and social security number of a valid employee is displayed for the operator's verification. After approval, the portion of the employee record dealing with pay is tested by the program at line 1220. If this is an *hourly* employee, the hourly and overtime rates of pay are displayed. If this is an employee paid a *fixed salary*, this fact and the rate of pay are displayed. The point to be made here is that there are two different ways of calculating the gross pay. A salaried employee is paid the full salary for 40 hours of work, and proportionately less for less than 40 hours. An hourly employee is paid straight time for up to 40 hours, and at some other rate for overtime hours. How these matters are handled is subject to variation among employers, and some aspects are rigidly controlled by the National Labor Relations Board. Employers should seek assurance from their accountants that their methods are proper. Any necessary changes can

Program Listing 7-2. "PAYDAY"

```
1000 REM PAY PROGRAM PAYDAY-NORTH STAR BASIC REL.4
1010 DIM N$(20),S$(13)\El=750\REM STANDARD DEDUCTION
1020 REM El=$ EXEMPTION PER DEDUCTION
1030 PRINT CHR$(27)+"*"
1040 PRINT"*****PAYDAY*****"
1050 INPUT"ENTER PAYROLL PERIOD END AS MM.DD ",Dl
1060 IF INT(Dl)<1 OR INT(Dl)>12 THEN 1050
1070 IF 100*(Dl-INT(Dl))<1 OR 100*(Dl-INT(Dl))>31 THEN 1050
1080 PRINT\PRINT"INPUT HOURS WORKED. PAY AND DEDUCTIONS WILL"
1090 PRINT"BE CALCULATED AND PRINTED, WITH Y.T.D. FIGURES"
1100 PRINT\OPEN#1,"EMPDATA"\READ#1%0,L
1110 PRINT\PRINT"INPUT PAY NUMBER OF EMPLOYEE OR 0 TO END ",
1120 INPUT Q\IF Q=0 THEN CHAIN"PAYMENU"
1125 IF Q<1 THEN 1110
1130 IF Q>L THEN PRINT"OUT OF RANGE"\IF Q>L THEN 1110
1140 PRINT CHR$(12)\REM YOUR CLEAR SCREEN CHARACTER
1145 GOSUB 1330\REM READ EMPL.RECORD
1150 El=0\Hl=0\S3=0\F3=0\F4=0\O2=0\O4=0\N1=0
1160 IF E<0 THEN PRINT"NO EMPLOYEE WITH THAT NUMBER"
1170 IF E>0 THEN 1190
1180 GOTO 1110
1190 GOSUB 1360\REM DISPLAY EMPLOYEE DATA
1200 PRINT\INPUT"CORRECT EMPLOYEE (Y/N)",Q$
1210 IF Q$="N"THEN 1110
1220 IF S1>0 THEN 1250
1230 PRINT"HOURLY",%7F2,H, TAB(25),"OVERTIME ",%7F2,O
1240 GOTO 1260
1250 PRINT"SALARIED EMPLOYEE ",%8F2,S1," PER WEEK"
1260 PRINT\INPUT"HOURS WORKED THIS WEEK ",Hl
1265 IF Hl<0 OR Hl>100 THEN 1260
1270 REM FIGURE PERCENTAGE OF FULL PAY
1280 IF S1>0 THEN G1=S1*(Hl/40)\REM SALARY
1290 IF S1>0 THEN 1390
1300 IF Hl>40 THEN 1320\REM IF OVERTIME
1310 G1=Hl*H \GOTO 1390\REM PAY FOR 40 OR LESS HRS
1320 H2=Hl-40\G1=(H*40)+(H2*O)\GOTO 1390
1330 READ#1%Q*100,E\IF E<0 THEN RETURN
1340 READ#1%Q*100,E,N$,S$,M$,D,S1,H,O,G,F1,S2,F2,O1,O3,N
1350 RETURN
1360 REM PLACE YOUR CLEAR SCREEN CHARACTER HERE"
1370 PRINT\PRINT"   EMPLOYEE #",%4I,E,
1380 PRINT N$,TAB(25)," ",S$\RETURN
1390 G2=G1\REM CALCULATIONS BEGIN HERE
1400 REM G1 IS GROSS PAY REGARDLESS HOW EARNED
1410 G1=G1*52\REM TO ANNUALIZE PAY
1420 REM COMPUTE GROSS AFTER DEDUCTIONS
1430 G1=G1-(D*El)\REM El IS STANDARD EXEMPTION
1440 REM G1 IS NOW ANNUAL PAY LESS STANDARD DEDUCTIONS
1450 INPUT"OTHER DEDUCTION 1 (OR 0) ",O2
1460 INPUT"OTHER DEDUCTION 2 (OR 0) ",O4
1470 REM BEGIN TAX TABLES
1480 REM FOR MONTANA TAX WHETHER SINGLE OR MARRIED
1490 IF G1>35000 THEN S3=(G1-35000)*.121+3135
1500 IF G1>20000 AND G1<35000 THEN S3=(G1-20000)*.11+1485
1510 IF G1>14000 AND G1<20000 THEN S3=(G1-14000)*.099+891
1520 IF G1>10000 AND G1<14000 THEN S3=(G1-10000)*.088+539
1530 IF G1>8000  AND G1<10000 THEN S3=(G1-8000)*.077+385
1540 IF G1>6000  AND G1<8000  THEN S3=(G1-6000)*.066+253
```

Program Listing 7–2 (cont)

```
1550 IF Gl>4000   AND Gl<6000   THEN S3=(Gl-4000)*.055+143
1560 IF Gl>2000   AND Gl<4000   THEN S3=(Gl-2000)*.044+55
1570 IF Gl>1000   AND Gl<2000   THEN S3=(Gl-1000)*.033+22
1580 IF Gl>0      AND Gl<1000   THEN S3=Gl*.022
1590 REM ANNUALIZED STATE TAX IS S3
1600 S3=S3/52\REM S3 IS NOW IN WEEKLY FORM
1610 REM F3 IS CURRENT FED TAX,F4 CURRENT FICA,N1=CUR NET
1620 IF M$="M" THEN 1730\REM IF MARRIED
1630 REM FEDERAL TAX IF SINGLE EMPLOYEE
1640 IF Gl>35000 THEN F3=(Gl-35000)*.39+9504
1650 IF Gl>20000 AND Gl<35000 THEN F3=(Gl-20000)*.34+4320
1660 IF Gl>14000 AND Gl<20000 THEN F3=(Gl-14000)*.28+2640
1670 IF Gl>10000 AND Gl<14000 THEN F3=(Gl-10000)*.24+1400
1680 IF Gl>8000  AND Gl<10000 THEN F3=(Gl-8000)*.22+1150
1690 IF Gl>4000  AND Gl<8000  THEN F3=(Gl-4000)*.20+168
1700 IF Gl>2500  AND Gl<4000  THEN F3=(Gl-2500)*.10+24
1710 IF Gl<2500  THEN F3=0
1720 F3=F3/52\GOTO 1830
1730 REM FEDERAL TAX IF MARRIED EMPLOYEE
1740 IF Gl>35000 THEN F3=(Gl-35000)*.37+11304
1750 IF Gl>20000 AND Gl<35000 THEN F3=(Gl-20000)*.33+3456
1760 IF Gl>14000 AND Gl<20000 THEN F3=(Gl-14000)*.27+2088
1770 IF Gl>12000 AND Gl<14000 THEN F3=(Gl-12000)*.24+1680
1780 IF Gl>8000  AND Gl<12000 THEN F3=(Gl-8000)*.2+888
1790 IF Gl>4000  AND Gl<8000  THEN F3=(Gl-4000)*.15+240
1800 IF Gl>2500  AND Gl<4000  THEN F3=(Gl-2500)*.10+24
1810 IF Gl>0     AND Gl<2500  THEN F3=0
1820 F3=F3/52\REM NOW IN WEEKLY FORM
1830 REM CALCULATE FICA
1840 F5=.0613\REM FICA PERCENT OF GROSS
1850 F7=25900\REM EARNINGS SUBJECT TO FICA
1860 F6=F5*F7\REM MAX TO BE DEDUCTED
1870 IF F2>=F6 THEN 1910
1880 F4=F5*G2\REM CURRENT FICA
1890 IF F4+F2<=F6 THEN 1910
1900 F8=(F4+F2)-F6\F4=F4-F8
1910 REM F4 IS FICA FOR THIS PERIOD
1920 REM
1930 Gl=G2\REM BACK TO WEEKLY FIGURE
1940 N1=G2-(F3+S3+F4+O2+O4)\REM N1 IS NET PAY
1950 REM
1960 REM FOLLOWING CAN BE MODIFIED TO PRINT CHECKS
1970 REM PAYDAY PRINT BEGINS HERE
1980 FOR X=1 TO 5\PRINT#1,CHR$(10)\NEXT
1990 PRINT#1,"EMP.#:", E,TAB(10),N$,TAB(31),S$," FOR",%6F2,D1,
1995 PRINT#1,TAB(59),H1," HOURS"
2000 PRINT#1,TAB(11),"GROSS",TAB(18),"FED W.T.",TAB(31),
2010 PRINT#1,"STATE "     ,TAB(41)," FICA",TAB(49),"OTHER-1",
2020 PRINT#1,TAB(59),"OTHER-2",TAB(69),"NET PAY"
2030 FOR X=1 TO 77\PRINT#1,"-",\NEXT\PRINT#1,"-"
2040 PRINT#1,"CUR *:",%10F2,G2,F3,S3,F4,O2,O4,N1
2050 G=G+G2\F1=F1+F3\S2=S2+S3\F2=F2+F4\O1=O1+O2\O3=O3+O4
2060 N=N+N1
2070 WRITE#1%Q*100,E,N$,S$,M$,D,S1,H,O,G,F1,S2,F2,O1,O3,N
2080 PRINT#1,"Y.T.D:",%10F2,G,F1,S2,F2,O1,O3,N
2090 FOR X=1 TO 77\PRINT#1,"=",\NEXT\PRINT#1,"="
2100 CLOSE#1\GOTO 1100
```

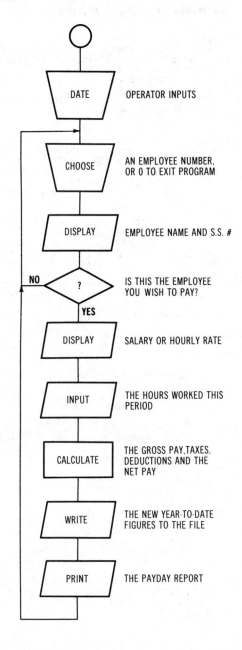

Fig. 7–3. Flowchart of the program, "PAYDAY."

be made in the program segment, lines 1220–1320. The pay procedure can be summarized as follows:

1. Open "PAYDAY" program; call for and verify first employee record.
2. Program accesses employee record for rate and exemptions.
3. Fill in requested information; that is, hours, exemptions, etc. (At this point, the program is ready to calculate pay and deductions. Calculations begin at line 1390.)
4. Program calculates the federal tax.
5. Program calculates the state tax.
6. Program calculates the FICA tax, first making sure that the maximum has not been exceeded for the year to date.

The final portion of any payroll operation consists of *printing the calculations*, either as a list or on the checks and stubs themselves. In the example program, the information is produced as a printed list from which checks may be written. To continue:

7. Program calculates any other deductions required.
8. Program prints the payday report.
9. Program updates the year-to-date records.
10. Repeat steps 1 through 9 for all employees.
11. Close the file and exit the "PAYDAY" program.

Example 7-3 shows the report that is generated as a result of the "PAYDAY" program. As noted, larger systems print the check at this point, and later will print other historical data. It is possible to print items such as the employee's W-2 form at the end of the year, and large payroll systems do so. Other business activities might require quarterly or yearly recaps of earnings, to aid in manual reporting.

Example 7-3. The Payday Report

EMP.#: 1	JOHN Q. TECH			123-45-6789		FOR 12.25	40 HOURS
	GROSS	FED W.T.	STATE	FICA	OTHER-1	OTHER-2	NET PAY
CUR :	150.00	17.85	7.15	9.20	5.00	.00	110.81
Y.T.D.:	975.00	98.54	54.27	44.18	6.00	3.00	869.01

EMP.#: 2	SUZY SALESPERSON			517-12-1429		FOR 12.25	44 HOURS
	GROSS	FED W.T.	STATE	FICA	OTHER-1	OTHER-2	NET PAY
CUR :	276.00	41.98	17.80	16.92	.00	.00	·199.29
Y.T.D.:	666.00	75.98	60.37	31.92	3.00	4.00	421.73

The report in the "PAYDAY" program is printed by lines 1960 onward. If the user wishes to have checks and stubs printed at this time, these are the only lines that need to be changed.

PAYROLL SUMMARY

Let us assume that a master file exists and that the tax tables are part of the calculation program. The operating procedure will then be:

1. Run the program, "PAYDAY."
2. When it prompts for an employee number, enter the number of the first employee to be processed.
3. The program opens the master file, finds the correct employee, and reads his or her data into the program.
4. If no such employee exists, an error message will be printed and the operator tries again.
5. If the correct employee has been identified, the program will next ask for the hours worked and the operator will enter the information.
6. Having the hours worked and the data from the employee file, the program will calculate:
   a. Gross pay.
   b. Withholding for tax and other purposes.
   c. The net pay (gross minus deductions).
7. The program then types this information on the printer.

CONCLUSION

As shown here, perhaps the payroll programs seem like any other, and our earlier pessimism about them might appear unfounded. In real life, problems arise because of the amount of detail involved. Payrolls have the nasty habit of working perfectly for weeks, or months, and then generating an unexpected error. This usually occurs when some circumstance is first encountered that has not previously been calculated and tested.

The frequent changes in tax tables and/or the formulae for calculating taxes were mentioned briefly. All such changes are a possible source of error. Another is the FICA deduction, which will come to an end (for some employees) at some time during the employee's pay year, usually between pay periods. As more items are added to the employee file—union checkoffs, savings plans, insurance, etc.—the chance of error increases. Overtime work is easy to account for, but less than a normal week can throw the procedures off the track, as can vacation, sick leave, and any special pluses or minuses to the "standard" work week and paycheck.

Our best advice for prospective payroll users is to buy the best program available for their particular size and type of business, and then modify it, or have it modified, to meet specifications. Avoid computer payrolls completely unless they are warranted by volume.

SELF-HELP TEST QUESTIONS

1. Name three possible causes of error in a computerized payroll system.

2. Can a computer print checks?

3. How are tax deductions calculated?

4. What kind of information is needed each time the payroll is calculated?

5. How would you decide if computerizing your payroll was worthwhile?

TEST PROGRAMMING PROJECT

Carefully review the text of this chapter and the payroll programs listed herein. Obtain federal and state tax tables and write the necessary program lines to make these calculations. It may be necessary to add additional lines depending on the detail you wish to calculate.

As an alternate project, draw a "dummy" check on a piece of printer paper and rearrange the PRINT lines in the "PAYDAY" program so that they will print the pay information on the "check." You may also wish to print a facsimile of a check stub that will inform the employee of year-to-date earnings and deductions.

8

General Ledger Programs

OBJECTIVES

In this chapter the reader will become acquainted with the following:

- The principles of double-entry accounting.
- The makeup of general ledger systems as they are used in business computing.
- A modest general ledger package for small businesses.

TERMS DEFINED

Double-Entry Accounting—An accounting system in which each transaction is represented by two or more entries. For example, a cash sale is recorded as an increase in the account called *cash* and a decrease in the account called *merchandise for sale*. It is a nearly universal system which originated in thirteenth-century Europe.

Account—A classification of items having a common function in the business. Cash can enter the business or go out of the business; therefore, "cash" is an account name in which these events are listed.

Account Number—In addition to being named, all accounts are numbered. The numbering follows a logical plan, and the assigned numbers have special meaning in the system.

Chart of Accounts—The list of account names and numbers is called the chart of accounts.

Transaction—Any exchange of goods, services, or money.

Debit and Credit—These terms represent two columns in an account book. Depending upon which account is being discussed, either column can represent an increase or a decrease. Examples will be given later in the chapter.

Journal, or *Transaction File*—The chronological listing of transactions, either in a book or a data file.

Ledgers and *Posting*—In contrast with the journal, ledgers have transaction entries grouped by account number. Posting is the term that refers to transcribing the entries from the journal to the ledgers. Ledger accounts may also be in book form or in the form of a data file.

Financial Reports—Information derived from the ledgers and arranged in a form that has meaning to the business. The *profit-and-loss statement* and the *balance sheet* are the main financial reports. Sales or other special-purpose reports may be important to some businesses.

GENERAL LEDGER DEFINED

In computer work, the expression *general ledger* refers to the accounts themselves, the entries in them, and reports that may be derived from the raw data. We find some very complex general ledger program packages, and some that are extremely simple.

In large systems, the transaction file and ledgers may communicate directly with other program elements, such as the payroll, and an impressive quantity of reports may be generated. In small business systems, the term usually means, at the least, the *transaction file*, the *ledger accounts* into which transactions are eventually posted, and some minimum volume of *financial reporting*. In some systems, the financial reports are entirely missing.

The essential actions of the small system are:

1. Record the transactions as they occur.
2. Post them to the ledgers at the end of the accounting period.
3. Provide some kind of listing of transactions, or of ledger totals, sufficient for the manual compilation of financial reports; or, in some cases, prepare the simpler reports automatically.

The set of programs to be developed and listed in this chapter will perform the most essential functions, and the reporting can either be added to the set, as described later, or manually prepared from the existing totals.

SYSTEM OVERVIEW

It should be no surprise to learn that the system will involve data files on disk. There will be two such files that are manipulated by three separate programs. Fig. 8-1 illustrates the system concept. In addition to the main files there will be a third, temporary file (TEMP) used in a sorting process. The printouts produced by the system are the chart of accounts, the raw transactions printed for editing purposes, and the ledgers, which are the sorted version of the raw transactions.

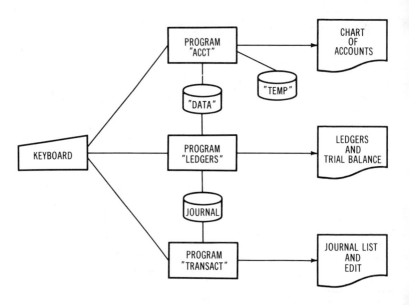

Fig. 8–1. General ledger system diagram.

Chart of Accounts

The program, "ACCT," services the chart of accounts. This function is basically a rather simple information storage and retrieval process. The only difference between this program and similar programs already covered is the sorting function that is included here. The accounts must always be in ascending numerical order, and adding a new account requires a reorganization of the file to place the new one in proper order. The function is automatic.

Transaction File

The program, "TRANSACT," is also a storage and retrieval function. In this instance, the entries, made from the keyboard, are the transactions. Each entry consists of the proper account number, the date, the description or reference document, and an amount in either the debit or credit column. The entries are made by the operator from the keyboard.

At the end of an accounting period, usually a calendar month, the transaction file is read by the program and the entries are grouped by account number, rather than in their originally entered random order. The program, "LEDGERS," does this and at the same time prints the sorted results. Posting to the ledgers from the transaction file is an automatic function. The ledger account totals are the basis for financial reporting.

TRANSACTION EXAMPLES

There may well be dozens, or scores, of accounts in even a small business. For illustration, let us assume that three of these accounts are numbered 101, 102, and 110. Their names are "CASH," "ACCOUNTS RECEIVABLE," and "MERCHANDISE." Some imaginary transactions will be made to demonstrate the accounting methods under discussion. Example 8-1 represents a cash transaction—the sale of merchandise for cash.

Example 8-1. A Sample Entry for a Cash Sale

	DEBIT	CREDIT
101 CASH SALE	12.50	.00
110 SOLD	.00	12.50

Two *entries* were required for the one *transaction*. Cash was increased and merchandise decreased. In both of these accounts, increases are recorded in the debit column. This is not true for all account classifications. The rules for debits and credits can be found in accounting textbooks.

A second transaction is now recorded. In this case, the merchandise is charged. Example 8-2 demonstrates the use of the accounts-receivable classification. An *account receivable* is money owed the business. In this way, sales or other revenues are "accrued," or added to the books, even though no money has yet changed hands.

Example 8-2. A Sample Entry for a Charge Sale

	DEBIT	CREDIT
102 MR. CUSTOMER	15.00	.00
110 SOLD TO MR. CUSTOMER	.00	15.00

This decreased merchandise as before, but the debit this time is to accounts receivable rather than cash. As far as the books are concerned, the sale is recorded and the money owed by Mr. Customer (if he is reliable) is the same as cash for purposes of financial reporting.

These two sales have removed $27.50 worth of merchandise from stock, so the business replaces it at a cost of $15.00 wholesale. This transaction is shown in Example 8-3.

Example 8-3. A Sample Entry for a Purchase

	DEBIT	CREDIT
101 MERCHANDISE	.00	15.00
110 BOUGHT FOR CASH	15.00	.00

Notice that this is exactly the reverse of the first example; cash has now been credited and merchandise (110) has been debited.

These isolated transactions would in real life appear as in Example 8-4, listed in the transaction file in the order in which they occurred.

Example 8-4. Printout of a Transaction File

	DEBIT	CREDIT
101 CASH SALE	15.00	.00
110 SOLD	.00	− 15.00
102 MR. CUSTOMER	12.50	.00
110 SOLD TO MR. CUS-TOMER	.00	− 12.50
101 MERCHANDISE	.00	− 15.00
110 BOUGHT FOR CASH	15.00	.00

Finally, as in Example 8-5, the six example entries, representing three transactions, would be sorted and arranged in ascending order of account numbers.

Example 8-5. A Set of Sorted Transactions

CASH	DEBIT	CREDIT	BALANCE
101 CASH SALE	15.00	.00	15.00
101 MERCHANDISE	.00	15.00	.00
ACCOUNTS RECEIVABLE			
102 MR. CUSTOMER	12.50	.00	12.50
MERCHANDISE			
110 SOLD	.00	15.00	− 15.00
110 SOLD TO MR. CUS-TOMER	.00	12.50	− 27.50
110 BOUGHT FOR CASH	15.00	.00	− 12.50
PROOF =			....0.00

And a third column of figures has been added—the *balance*. This is optional and is not found in all ledger systems. Notice, also, that credit balances show as negative numbers. Line 1390 of the program, "TRANSACT," takes care of this conversion at the time the transaction is entered.

The final point to be made by Examples 8-1, 2, 3, 4, and 5 is the concept of balanced books. If all the credits in Example 8-4 (or in Example 8-5) are added together, the total is $42.50 and the same figure is obtained by adding all of the debits. The books are now said to be *balanced*. Taking these totals is referred to as the *proof* or the *trial balance*. In a computerized system, the program does this automatically by accumulating a running total while it posts the transactions to the ledgers. The theory behind this is that it is nearly impossible to make two identical errors; therefore, an unbalanced condition will have detected an error condition that warrants further investigation.

PROGRAM DESCRIPTIONS

Program "ACCT"

As it is essential to the entire general ledger process, the chart of accounts program will be analyzed first. Program "ACCT" is written in North Star BASIC, Release 4. Sections will be referenced both by the flowchart, Fig. 8-2, and by line numbers within the program itself, Program Listing 8-1.

First observe the flowchart. It begins with symbolic notation enabling the operator to choose the activity desired, and enabling the program to decide which course of action to implement. Line numbers 1000 through 1090 perform these functions. The choices are:

1. Create a new file (list of accounts).
2. Reorganize the chart of accounts.
3. Add a new account.
4. Print a list of the accounts.
5. Delete an account.

Creating a new file is accomplished by lines 1780 through 1850. This module creates a fixed-length file called "DATA" and another called "TEMP," and writes a -1 in each record space. The program will recognize each -1 entry as being an empty file space.

Entering data for each account to be used is accomplished by lines 1100 to 1260. The operator will be prompted to enter each item of information. Upon approval of the completed record, it will be written in the file.

An existing account can be deleted by the routine at lines 1280 through 1330. The account is deleted by writing a -2 in the file space. The program will be able to recognize this as a deleted record and skip over it.

Lines 1440 through 1760 reorganize the file by sorting the records into ascending account number order and writing over the deleted spaces. This routine is completely automatic when the option is selected, but its technique warrants some explanation.

The main file, "DATA," is first read into file "TEMP" exactly as is. At the same time, the account numbers and the address within the file are read into arrays. Following this transfer, the arrays are sorted using what is known as a *bubble sort*. This rather slow, rather simple method works by comparing two adjacent account numbers and exchanging them if they are in "wrong" order. At the same time, the file addresses are also swapped. After this, the records are read, in sorted order, from "TEMP," and written back to the file, "DATA." The remaining file space is then reinitialized with the -1 value. This system works well for a few dozen entries; much larger charts of accounts can benefit from a faster method of sorting.

The routine at lines 1350 through 1410 simply reads all the valid entries and lists them on the printer. This is done to provide a permanent listing and also to verify, from time to time, that the accounts are in order. The print routine is executed automatically following each reorganization.

Program "TRANSACT"

The flowchart (Fig. 8-3) and Program Listing 8-2 will be referenced in describing the entering and editing of individual transactions. In addition to making entries, the operator may also choose to print all existing entries for editing purposes. If mistakes are detected, there is an option for making a correction. This option reads and displays the

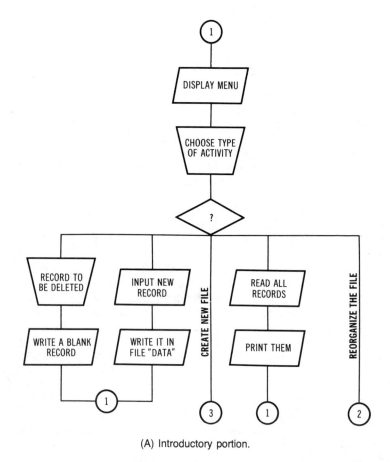

(A) Introductory portion.

Fig. 8-2. Flowchart of

desired record and writes it back to the same place in the file after new data have been provided. These entries (transactions) will normally be made in the order in which they occur. There is also an option to create a new file; this portion of the program works in a manner similar to the "CREATE" routine described earlier for the chart of accounts.

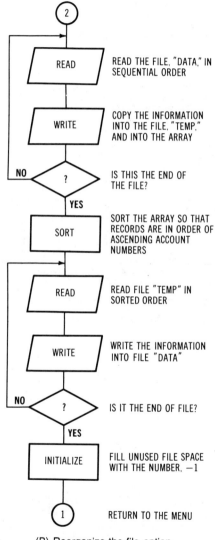

(B) Reorganize-the-file option.

the program, "ACCT."

Program Listing 8–1. "ACCT"

```
1000 REM PROGRAM ACCT-NORTH STAR BASIC REL.4
1010 DIM N$(15),A(25,2)
1020 PRINT CHR$(12)\REM CLEAR SCREEN CHAR
1030 PRINT"CHART OF ACCOUNTS"\PRINT
1040 PRINT"1) ADD AN ACCOUNT"\PRINT"2) DELETE AN ACCOUNT"
1050 PRINT"3) LIST ACCOUNTS"\PRINT"4) REORGANIZE FILE"
1060 PRINT"5) CREATE NEW FILE "\PRINT
1070 REM
1080 INPUT"SELECT BY NBR ",Q\IFQ<1 OR Q>5 THEN 1080
1090 ON Q GOTO 1100,1280,1360,1440,1780
1100 OPEN#1,"DATA"\READ#1%0,R2
1110 INPUT"ACCOUNT NBR (100-999) ",A
1120 IF A<100 OR A>999 THEN 1110
1130 INPUT"ACCOUNT NAME(15 CHAR) ",N$
1140 IF LEN(N$)>15 THEN N$=N$(1,15)
1150 INPUT"ACCOUNT TYPE(0-3)        ",T
1160 IF T<0 OR T>3 OR T<>INT(T) THEN 1150
1170 INPUT"NORMAL BALANCE(DR/CR) ",B$
1180 IF B$="CR" THEN 1200\IF B$="DR" THEN 1200
1190 GOTO 1170
1200 PRINT\PRINT R2+1,A,T," ",N$," ",B$\PRINT
1210 INPUT"FILE IT  (Y/N) ",Q$
1220 IF Q$<>"Y" THEN 1020
1230 REM
1240 REM WRITE IN FILE AND ALSO SET FILE LENGTH
1250 WRITE#1%40*(R2+1),A,T,N$,B$\WRITE#1%0,R2+1
1260 CLOSE#1\GOTO 1020
1270 REM
1280 PRINT\INPUT"DELETION ROUTINE. CONTINUE (Y/N) ",Q$
1290 IF Q$="Y" THEN 1300 ELSE 1020
1300 OPEN#1,"DATA"\READ#1%0,R2
1310 INPUT"RECORD NBR TO DELETE ",Q
1320 IF Q<>INT(Q) OR Q<0 OR Q>R2 THEN 1260
1330 WRITE#1%Q*40,-2\CLOSE#1\GOTO 1020
1340 REM
1350 REM READ AND PRINT THE CHART OF ACCOUNTS
1360 OPEN#1,"DATA"\READ#1%0,R2
1370 FOR X=1 TO R2
1380     READ#1%X*40 ,A\IF A<100 THEN 1410
1390     READ#1%X*40,A,T,N$,B$
1400     PRINT#1,%4I,A,T," ",N$,TAB(30),"NORMAL BAL=",B$
1410 NEXT X\CLOSE#1\GOTO 1020
1420 REM
1430 REM TRANSFER TO WORK FILE
1440 OPEN#1,"DATA"\OPEN#2,"TEMP"\READ#1%0,R2
1450 FOR X=1 TO R2\READ#1%X*40,A
1460     IF A<0 THEN 1500
1470     READ#1%X*40,A,T,N$,B$
1480     A(X,1)=X\A(X,2)=A
1490     WRITE#2%X*40,A,T,N$,B$
1500 NEXT X
```

Program Listing 8–1 (cont)

```
1510 REM
1520 REM SORT THE ARRAY
1530 PRINT"SORTING....DO NOT DISTURB"
1540 FOR X=1 TO 25
1550     FOR Y=1 TO 24
1560     IF A(Y,2)<0 THEN 1610
1570     A=A(Y,2)\B=A(Y,1)
1580     IF A<A(Y+1,2) THEN 1610
1590     A(Y,2)=A(Y+1,2)\A(Y,1)=A(Y+1,1)
1600     A(Y+1,2)=A\A(Y+1,1)=B
1610 NEXT Y\NEXT X
1620 REM
1630 REM WRITE BACK TO MAIN FILE
1640 Z=1
1650 FOR X=1 TO 25
1660     IF A(X,2)<100 THEN 1690
1670     READ#2%40*A(X,1),A,T,N$,B$
1680     WRITE#1%Z*40,A,T,N$,B$\Z=Z+1
1690 NEXT X
1700 REM RE-INITIALIZE THE FILES
1710 FOR X=Z TO 25
1720     WRITE#1%X*40,-1
1730 NEXT X
1740 FOR X= 1 TO 25
1750     WRITE#2%X*40,-1
1760 NEXT X\GOTO 1370
1770 REM
1780 CREATE"DATA",4\CREATE"TEMP",4
1790 OPEN#1,"DATA"\OPEN#2,"TEMP"
1800 FOR X=1 TO 25
1810     WRITE#1%X*40,-1
1820     WRITE#2%X*40,-1
1830 NEXT X
1840 WRITE#1%0,0\WRITE#2%0,0
1850 CLOSE#1\CLOSE#2\GOTO 1020
```

New files are created when the program is first put in use and whenever a new accounting period demands that the records be deleted and a new set of data accumulated.

Program "LEDGERS"

Program "LEDGERS" differs in several ways from the more-or-less standard storage and retrieval functions we have been discussing. One major difference is that it operates simultaneously with *two* data files—the *chart of accounts* and the *transaction file*.

"LEDGERS" is a short, simple program that nevertheless performs major functions entirely without help from the operator. Fig. 8-4 is the flowchart of "LEDGERS." In this program, the operator is given two options—to print the entire ledger system or to print the entries in any one particular ledger account.

First, observe the option to print a selected account. This is accomplished by lines 1130 through 1300 in Program Listing 8-3. The operator is prompted to input the account number. The program then

Program Listing 8–2. "TRANSACT"

```
1000 REM PROGRAM TRANSACT-NORTH STAR BASIC REL.4
1010 R=50\REM R IS EXPECTED NUMBER OF RECORDS
1020 DIM N$(15),B$(2),I$(15)
1030 INPUT"ENTER DATE AS MM.DD ",D
1040 IF INT(D)<0 OR INT(D)>12 THEN 1030
1050 IF 100*(D-INT(D))<1 OR 100*(D-INT(D))>31 THEN 1030
1060 OPEN#2,"DATA"\READ#2%0,L
1070 PRINT CHR$(12)\REM YOUR CLEAR SCREEN CHAR HERE
1080 PRINT"G/L TRANSACTIONS"\PRINT
1090 PRINT"1. MAKE AN ENTRY"
1100 PRINT"2. CORRECTIONS"
1110 PRINT"3. TOTAL AND BALANCE"
1120 PRINT"4. CREATE A NEW FILE"
1130 PRINT\INPUT"SELECT BY NBR ",Q
1140 IF Q<1 OR Q>4 OR Q<>INT(Q) THEN 1130
1150 IF Q=4 THEN 1640
1160 OPEN#1,"JOURNAL"\READ#1%0,R1
1170 ON Q GOTO 1190,1200,1510
1180 REM
1190 R=R1+1\GOTO 1250
1200 INPUT"RECORD # TO CHANGE, 0 IF FINISHED",R
1210 IF R=0 THEN CLOSE#1\IF R=0 THEN 1070
1220 IF R<1 OR R>R1 OR R<>INT(R) THEN 1200
1230 GOSUB 1500
1240 GOTO 1400
1250 PRINT"ENTER ACCOUNT # OR 0 IF FINISHED"
1260 INPUT "ACCOUNT # ",A
1270 IF A=0 THEN CLOSE#1\IF A=0 THEN 1090
1280 IF A<100 OR A>999 THEN 1260
1290 FOR X=1 TO L\READ#2%X*40,A1
1300 IF A1=A THEN EXIT 1320\NEXT X
1310 PRINT"ACCOUNT # NOT ON FILE"\GOTO 1190
1320 READ#2%X*40,A1,T,N$,B$\PRINT
1330 PRINT A1," ",N$," TYPE",T," NORMAL ",B$," BALANCE"
1340 PRINT\PRINT
1350 INPUT"CORRECT (Y/N) ",Q$\IF Q$="Y" THEN 1370
1360 GOTO 1260\PRINT\PRINT
1370 INPUT"ITEM   :",I$
1380 INPUT"DEBIT  :",D1
1390 INPUT"CREDIT:",C1\C1=C1*(-1)
1400 PRINT CHR$(12)\REM YOUR CLR SCREEN CHAR HERE
1410 PRINT A1,          TAB(19),N$,TAB(40),"DEBIT     CREDIT"
1420 FOR X=1 TO 60\PRINT"."\NEXT X\PRINT"."
1430 PRINTD, TAB(13),I$,TAB(35),%10F2,D1,C1
1440 PRINT\PRINT\PRINT
1450 INPUT"APPROVED (Y/N)",Q$\IF Q$<>"Y" THEN 1370
1460 IF Q=2 THEN 1480
1470 WRITE#1%0,R
1480 WRITE#1%R*50,A1,D,I$,D1,C1
1490 CLOSE#1\GOTO 1160
1500 READ#1%R*50, A1,D,I$,D1,C1\RETURN
```

Program Listing 8–2 (cont)

```
1510 B=0\REM TOTAL AND BALANCE
1520 PRINT"REC-ACCT DATE          ITEM                    DR        CR"
1530 PRINT"        BAL"
1540 FOR R=1 TO R1
1550      GOSUB 1500
1560      B=B+C1+D1
1570      GOSUB 1610
1580 NEXT R
1590 INPUT"PRESS RETURN TO CONTINUE",Z$
1600 CLOSE#1\GOTO 1070
1610 FOR X=1 TO 60\PRINT".",\NEXT\PRINT"."
1620 PRINTR, A1,TAB(7),D,TAB(15),I$,TAB(33),%9F2,D1,C1,B
1630 RETURN
1640 REM CREATE FILE
1650 CREATE"JOURNAL",INT(R/5)\OPEN#1,"JOURNAL"
1660 FOR X=1 TO R
1670      WRITE#1%X*50,-1
1680 NEXT X
1690 WRITE#1%0,0\CLOSE#1\GOTO 1070
```

reads the chart of accounts (lines 1150–1190), searching for the account. If there is no such account, a message, "ACCOUNT NOT FOUND," is printed. After each search, the operator can ask for another account or enter an account number of zero to terminate the search. If the desired account exists, it is read and the account number and name are printed. The remaining lines of this module are then executed. The transaction file is read sequentially and the data for all matching account numbers is printed.

The second option is even more automatic than the first. The technique used here (lines 1320 through 1480) is to read the first account name and number from the chart of accounts, and then read and print all matching transaction entries. The next account number is treated similarly, and so on until all transaction entries have been printed with like account numbers grouped together in ascending order. Notice that this program is exclusively a read-and-print operation. No data is input by the operator and no writing in the files takes place. It should be noted that the printout of this function (shown in Example 8-7) is a larger version of Example 8-5, shown earlier in the chapter. This completes the program descriptions; their use by the operator in the course of normal business will be described next.

OPERATING THE GENERAL LEDGER SYSTEM

Chart of Accounts

A certain amount of planning should be done before placing the general ledger system in operation. The chart of accounts is a good place to start. All categories of *revenues*, *expenses*, *assets*, and *liabilities*

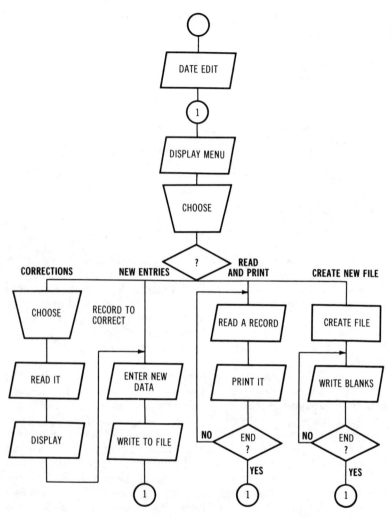

Fig. 8–3. Flowchart of the program, "TRANSACT."

should be listed and a numbering system established. As an example, all
assets should be placed in one number series, liabilities in another,
revenues in another, and expenses in yet another series. The numbers
should be large enough to provide room for expansion. Assets might be
numbered 100 through 199, expenses 200 through 299, and so forth.
Notice that the first digit tells us what class of account is intended.

Another classification is needed; this can be called the *report* type. As
a suggestion, those accounts dealing with profit-and-loss reports might

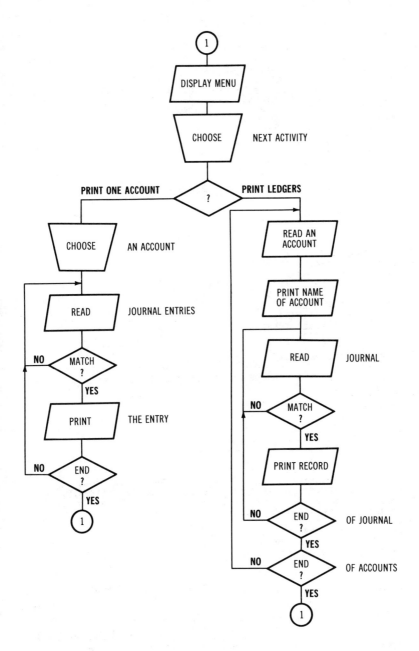

Fig. 8–4. Flowchart of the program, "LEDGERS."

Program Listing 8–3. "LEDGERS"

```
1000 REM PROGRAM LEDGERS-NORTH STAR BASIC REL.4
1010 DIM A$(15),N$(15),I$(15)
1020 OPEN#1,"DATA" \OPEN#2,"JOURNAL"
1030 READ#1%0,L\READ#2%0,L1
1040 PRINT CHR$(12)\REM YOUR CLEAR SCREEN CHARACTER HERE
1050 PRINT"LEDGERS"\PRINT
1060 PRINT"1. PRINT SELECTED ACCOUNT"
1070 PRINT"2. TOTAL AND TRIAL BALANCE"
1080 PRINT\INPUT "SELECT BY NBR ",Q
1090 IF Q<0 OR Q>2 OR Q<>INT(Q) THEN 1080
1100 REM
1110 ON Q GOTO 1130,1320
1120 REM PRINT A SELECTED LEDGER
1130 PRINT\INPUT"ACCOUNT NUMBER OR  0 TO TERMINATE ",Q
1140 IF Q=0 THEN 1040\IFQ<100 OR Q>999 THEN 1130
1150 FOR X=1 TO L
1160      READ#1%X*40,A
1170      IF A<0 THEN 1190
1180      IF A=Q THEN EXIT 1210
1190 NEXT X
1200 PRINT"ACCOUNT NOT FOUND"\GOTO 1040
1210 READ#1%X*40,A1,T,A$,B$
1220 PRINT#1,CHR$(10)
1230 PRINT#1,A1,TAB(10),A$\PRINT#1,CHR$(10)
1240 B=0
1250 FOR X=1 TO L1
1260      READ#2%X*50,A
1270      IF A1<>A THEN 1300
1280      READ#2%X*50,D,A, I$,D1,C1\B=B+D1+C1
1290      PRINT#1, D,TAB(7),A, TAB(14),I$,TAB(30),%10F2,D1,C1,B
1300 NEXT X\GOTO 1040
1310 REM
1320 REM PRINT ALL LEDGERS AND THEIR TOTALS
1330 B1=0\REM ACCUMULATE TOTALS
1340 FOR X=1 TO L\B=0
1350      READ#1%X*40,A1
1360      IF A1<0 THEN 1440
1370      READ#1%X*40,A1,T,A$,B$
1375      PRINT#1,A$,TAB(20),A1
1380      FOR Y=1 TO L1
1390           READ#2%Y*50,A
1400           IF A1<>A THEN 1430
1410           READ#2%Y*50,A,D, I$,D1,C1\B=B+D1+C1
1420      PRINT#1, D,TAB(7),A, TAB(14),I$,TAB(30),%10F2,D1,C1,B
1430      NEXT Y
1440 B1=B1+B\PRINT#1,CHR$(10)
1450 NEXT X
1460 PRINT#1,CHR$(10)\PRINT#1,TAB(35),
1470 PRINT#1,"TRIAL BALANCE=",TAB(55),%10F2,B1
1480 GOTO 1040
```

be coded 1, balance-sheet accounts 2, sales reports 3, and a zero in the field can indicate that no reports are involved. It should be noted that the accounts now have two "keys." The account number describes, in addition to the unique account itself, the general classification of revenue, expense, etc. The report field indicates the reports for which the account will provide data. If revenues are the 300 series, and expenses the 200 series, and they are both used in the profit-and-loss statement, this information will be "known" to the programs.

Within a series—that is, for example, 100 to 199—the accounts should be placed in the order you wish them to appear in the ledgers and reports. At this point, the chart of accounts may be entered into the file by program "ACCT." Before creating the file, an estimate should be made of the number of accounts that will be required. As written, the program initializes four sectors of file space. This provides for 24 accounts. An additional sector (256 bytes) is required for each additional six accounts; thus, if space for six more accounts is needed, the number of sectors (specified in line 1780 of program "ACCT") should be increased by one prior to creating the file.

The account entries permit an account number, account name, a field for the report type (which may be zero if not used), and a choice of debit or credit for the account's "normal" balance. The latter field is mostly for the operator's information and does not "do anything" to the data. Example 8-6 shows a typical entry in the chart of accounts.

Example 8-6. A Typical Entry in the Chart of Accounts

```
101 1    CASH    NORMAL BAL = DR
```

Account 101 is the "CASH" account, the report type is 1, and the account will normally have a debit (DR) balance.

After entering the accounts, the "reorganize" option should be run to assure they are in proper order; this action will also cause the chart to be printed out for reference.

Transactions

As each transaction occurs, or when several have been accumulated on paper, entries must be made in the transaction file, via program "TRANSACT." A decision will have been made about each transaction as to which accounts will be debited or credited. Entries can be made in the order in which the transactions take place, or in any order at all for that matter. At this point in the process, order is of no importance.

At the end of the period, a listing of all entries can be made from program "TRANSACT." This can be done as often as desired; it does not affect the entries in any way. As the entries are listed, the program will keep a running balance. If the balance indicates an error, the bad entry can be found and corrected from the same program.

Ledger Posting

The transaction entries can be sorted into the order determined by the chart of accounts at any time. The operator may wish to check all transactions to date in the cash account. This can be done by running "LEDGERS" and asking for the account by number. Any number of accounts can be viewed any number of times, with no change to the transaction file.

At the end of the accounting period, the operator will wish to have all accounts printed in their entirety. This printout will constitute the *posted ledgers* for the period. It is an automatic function set into motion simply by choosing that option of the program, "LEDGERS." Example 8-7 shows a comparison of the transaction information and the sorted ledger information.

Example 8-7. A Comparison of Sorted and Unsorted Transactions

(A) As Entered in Transaction File

REC- ACCT DATE		ITEM	DR	CR	BAL
1 101	12.14	DEC SALES	1205.32	.00	1205.32
2 110	12.14	DEC SALES, CASH	.00	−1205.32	.00
3 101	12.14	MISC EXPENSE	.00	−131.00	−131.00
4 201	12.14	OFFICE SUPPLIES	131.00	.00	.00
5 102	12.14	MR. CUSTOMER	99.95	.00	99.95
6 110	12.14	CHARGE SALE	.00	−99.95	.00
7 101	12.18	PD PHONE BILL	.00	−47.25	−47.25
8 201	12.18	TELEPHONE	47.25	.00	.00

(B) As Printed by Program "LEDGERS"

CASH IN BANK	101				
12.14	101	DEC SALES	1205.32	.00	1205.32
12.14	101	MISC EXPENSE	.00	−131.00	1074.32
12.18	101	PD PHONE BILL	.00	−47.25	1027.07

ACCT RECBL	102				
12.14	102	MR. CUSTOMER	99.95	.00	99.95

MERCHANDISE	110				
12.14	110	DEC SALES, CASH	.00	−1205.32	−1205.32
12.14	110	CHARGE SALE	.00	−99.95	−1305.27

MISC. EXPENSE	201				
12.14	201	OFFICE SUPPLIES	131.00	.00	131.00
12.18	201	TELEPHONE	47.25	.00	178.25

TRIAL BALANCE .00

Other Operating Activities

The transaction file is periodically destroyed after sorting and printing. Certain account balances must be carried forward to the next accounting period, and others are deliberately returned to a zero balance after making special entries for "adjusting" and "closing" the accounts. These are accounting functions and are to some extent business-dependent, and a thorough explanation is not possible in a book about programming. These actions should be worked out on an individual basis with the accountant responsible for the financial affairs of the business.

The only other remaining activity is the preparation of financial reports. The ledger set used here for demonstration of general ledger principles contains no such provision. This again is a matter of some choice and innovation by the individual user. Having the ledgers sorted and totaled enables relatively easy manual preparation of reports, as outlined in the following paragraphs.

Financial Reports

The most used reports are profit-and-loss reports and the balance sheet. Mention has already been made of identifying accounts by report type (1, 2, 3, or 0). In general, the profit-and-loss report will entail adding the total of all accounts in the 300 series (if that series represents revenues), which also have a report type of 1. If the 200 series of account numbers has been assigned to expenses, then all 200 series with report type of 1 will be read into the report as expenses. Merging the figures will result in a profit or a loss being shown. A balance sheet involves the series of accounts designated as assets and liabilities (and report type 2) in a similar manner. These reports (and others) should be determined by the individual accountant.

The programmer wishing to include reports in the general ledger set should be able to do so after getting this far into the subject. A fourth program must be added to the set; the existing file may be used or, when printing the ledgers, a separate shorter file may be generated which contains only the totals of the individual ledger accounts.

SELF-HELP TEST QUESTIONS

1. What purposes are served by a general ledger system?
2. What part does the chart of accounts play in this?
3. How does a program "know" which accounts to include in a financial report?
4. Which file contains the information about transactions?
5. What must be done when adding a new account to the chart of accounts?

TEST PROJECT

Design a program to work with those included in this chapter that will print financial reports. Make an outline and a flowchart. Work with an accountant, if necessary, to determine the report formats and the accounts to be included.

9

An Introduction to Word Processing

OBJECTIVES

This chapter deals with the leading edge of a technology that is supposed to revolutionize office work. It will touch briefly on the following:

- Typing without paper.
- Filing without paper.
- Instant mail.

But mostly, it will deal with the *word-processing* technology that is commonly available now for small computers, and at a price that nearly every business can afford.

WORD-PROCESSING FUNCTIONS

Word processing is a special form of data manipulation. It is not clearly defined, and some of its functions often go under different names, such as text editing, information management, and text formatting. The essential thing about any such "system" is that it involves computer processing of words and text in some form, as contrasted with number manipulation. The purpose of this, of course, is to apply the power of the computer to written matter. A well-known example is typesetting in newspaper offices. In recent years, this technology has completely changed the publishing industry by increasing speed and reducing both labor and material costs.

OFFICE OF THE FUTURE

The term *office of the future* is often used when word processing is mentioned. The developing concept is that ordinary written matter can be largely replaced with stored computer data which, in turn, can be recalled, modified, and/or transmitted (either electrically or on paper) as desired. As this movement gained momentum in the late 1970s, some manufacturers were promoting separate word-processing systems, while others were including the technology within their general-purpose computers. The latter method will probably prevail.

There is little, if any, difference between a computer for manipulating numbers and one for manipulating words, and the reader has probably already guessed that word processing in any of its many forms is, again, a form of information storage and retrieval. In this particular usage, the data (being words and other characters) are first of all entered into the computer, usually from the keyboard of the console, and "processed" in some manner at a later time, perhaps minutes later, but more likely hours, weeks, or months later depending on the material.

In the realm of small business, it is more economical to add a word-processing function by merely adding a special software package to the basic system, than to purchase a computer dedicated to word processing. This is a practical, economical approach to the problem and is especially so for the small business that may not make full-time use of its computer for any one, single purpose.

There is even some basis for speculating that the office copier will eventually be linked to the computer, enabling "documents" that have never seen print (except on a video screen) to be "cranked out" in any necessary quantity. This would, incidentally, replace both the typewriter and the computer printer. A further move in that direction is exemplified by a trend toward having word processors (if the term can be stretched that far) send data, such as letters, to distant offices over telephone lines. This sort of thing is well within the present technology, and its future adoption depends only on the attitude of potential users.

At the end of the 1970s, at least one manufacturer was selling an information management system accessible by up to 100 remote terminals, all sharing the data base of the "home office." It reportedly contained a complete English dictionary and fragments of foreign-language dictionaries. This marvelous device not only typed or otherwise transmitted documents, it also proofread them and corrected the operator's spelling.

Here again, the top technology is not affordable to all of us, but a lot of it is, in the small-business price range. Ordinary typing and document processing is perhaps the major paper task in small offices, and computerizing it is definitely affordable and worthwhile.

HARDWARE REQUIREMENTS

The small business wishing to include word processing in its computer installation must pay some attention to hardware selection.

Although the software package itself (there are several on the market) is relatively cheap, its usefulness depends on certain hardware features. One of these is the printer; although any printer will work for the purpose, a more presentable product is generated if both upper- and lower-case letters can be printed. Many of the cheaper printers do not permit lower-case letters.

Also, written information has a more pleasing appearance if typewriter-quality print fonts are available rather than the more common dot-matrix type. Printers that are of typewriter quality generally cost more, although some use has been made of used electric typewriters modified for computer control. These devices are usually in the same price range as the cheaper dot-matrix printers, but may not be as rugged or as long-lasting. One of their advantages is that such repairs as may be required from time to time fall in the category of typewriter repair rather than computer repair.

An even more important consideration is the video monitor on which the initial typing and the subsequent editing will be accomplished. On-screen editing depends on being able to "back up" the cursor in order to delete or correct material that is in error. Professional word processing software is capable of immediately accessing any part of the screen. For that matter it usually can access any part of the text, which has been written, stored on disk, and called back into memory to be modified or printed.

SUITABLE SOFTWARE

The features and qualities of a typical word processor for use with small computers will now be briefly described.

- Text can be typed on the screen, stored on disk, and retrieved later. At any point in its life the text may be modified or printed.
- By appropriate commands when printed, the text can be formatted into any line length, any number of lines per page, and any line spacing. The right margin is often justified. (This is generally accomplished by using computer-generated variable spacing between words. No words need be divided.)
- Headings are automatically centered, and titles may be carried forward so that all pages are titled and numbered.
- During editing (on the screen) words or letters may be inserted or deleted, the text "opening" or "closing" to permit the changes. Entire paragraphs may be moved. Words or sentences may be automatically located and changed. For example, a word that was consistently misspelled can be corrected once and the correction will take effect throughout the entire manuscript. Frequently used phrases may be represented symbolically by "XX" or some other

easily typed representation, and all are added in the correct place by a search-and-replace feature when the pages are printed.
- Separate files may be kept for often-used paragraphs; these may be combined to make up a semicustomized form letter.

Several software packages capable of these features can be purchased, ready to use, for less than $500.

Anyone who has ever omitted a word, or an entire line, from an otherwise perfect typing job knows that word-processing capability is well worth the small additional cost of the software and hardware neessary to turn out a perfect manuscript the first time. If good hardware is chosen from the very beginning for the general-purpose computer, word processing can be added later for only a few hundred dollars.

This book has dealt with the actual writing of several kinds of business software, and the reader may well ask why the word-processor package cannot also be written by the individual, rather than purchased. That is a reasonable question, and the answer is that many individuals have written their own programs—some good, some bad. Word-processing packages are usually written in *machine language*, and if the intent is just to get a workable program quickly and economically, purchasing one of the ready-made packages is the most effective solution. From time to time, computer magazines publish articles about word-processing or editing programs written by individuals. It is not a task for the beginning programmer, but it can be done.

As mentioned earlier, programs claiming some sort of editing capability are quite common. Caution must be used in that some of these are limited to editing single lines or data files, for example, and may be extremely clumsy when dealing with pages of manuscript.

It is worth noting that many video terminals have a form of editing built in; the text displayed on the screen can be changed at will and then dumped into the computer as a block. It can only handle one "screenful" at a time but is useful nevertheless. As always, the point of view of this book with regard to word-processing or editing software of any kind is to see it work before parting with any money.

Typical word-processing software is available from the following companies:

Electric Pencil   Requires CP/M operating system
Michael Schrayer Software, Inc. (except TRS-80 version).
Glendale, CA 91205

Magic Wand   Various versions available.
Small Business Applications, Inc.
Houston, TX 77006

Word Smith	Various versions available.
Micro Diversions, Inc.	
Vienna, VA 22180	
Word Star	Requires CP/M operating system;
MicroPro International Corp.	minimum 44K memory. Directly
San Rafael, CA 94901	applicable to most common terminals
	and printers.

TIME SHARING

This may be an appropriate time to mention time sharing as a feature of the business computer. A few years ago, before the advent of the low-priced microprocessor, it appeared that the future of computers would involve many terminals connected to a large processor. This was accomplished by means of having the computer repeatedly check each terminal for input, perform a part of its task, and then go to the next terminal. In most cases the effect on the individual user was such that he or she was not aware of not having exclusive use of the machine.

Time sharing is still very much alive, but the development of low-cost computers for individual use has nullified many of its advantages. Now that time sharing is becoming available for even very small computers, it is again worthwhile to consider this feature. Its use in the future will involve several users in the same office complex, or the same building, rather than users scattered over a state or group of states as was first envisioned. Properly used, this can permit several business functions to be carried out simultaneously.

10

Basic Computer Modeling and Simulation

OBJECTIVES

What is a computer simulation? Briefly, it is a computer program that duplicates the essentials of a real-life problem and "predicts" the outcome. Many games are simulations. It is possible for a business model to be either a simulation or an actual, after-the-fact record. Thus, this chapter is about the following:

- The purpose of simulation programs.
- The "break-even" business concept.
- How to predict future business results.
- Other uses of simulation in business.

THE BREAK-EVEN EXAMPLE

An excellent use of computer modeling is the calculation of the break-even point for a small business. Fig. 10-1 and Program Listing 10-1 illustrate a way of accomplishing this function, and the following paragraphs will describe what each step is actually accomplishing. The reader may wish to solve a simple problem of this type and get acquainted with the principle before going on to larger problems. Calculating the break-even point is a real-life problem that is widely taught in business management courses. Unfortunately, many business people neglect its use after completing their formal education or, perhaps, they feel that the manual method of accomplishing this profit projection is too time-consuming or inaccurate. The use of a computer simulation enables many different "scenarios" to be tried before settling on one course of action.

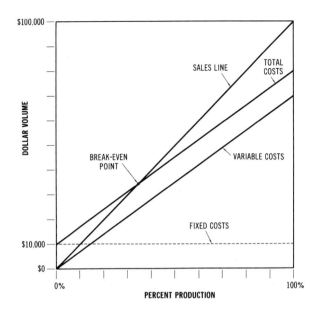

Fig. 10–1. A typical break-even chart.

To understand this project, assume that you have drawn a graph of your sales and expenses at the end of the month and, by connecting certain points on the graph or drawing lines from one point to another, you can analyze your profit margins and any "mistakes" that might have been made. Following the procedures used to make the graph shown in Fig. 10-1 will yield a model representing business activity for the month under consideration, and may reveal mistakes such as an overhead cost that is out of proportion to maximum sales or maximum production.

Fig. 10-1 is a graph describing a month's business for an imaginary company. The parameters are described by four straight lines; the *fixed costs* (rent, etc.), the *variable cost* at full production or sales (the difference between selling price and the cost, including commissions and other selling expenses), a third line representing *possible sales or production* from zero to 100%, and a fourth line which is the *sum of the fixed and variable costs*. By changing the values from which this graph was constructed, you can simulate changes in sales and expenses from zero to the maximum possible sales or production.

These are linear functions that could be solved mathematically by a single algebraic formula or by analytic geometry. In addition, the actual margin at any point on the sales line could be solved by hand or by using a pocket calculator. These methods, though, are limited to solving for only one set of variables at a time. The computer is not limited in this manner.

125

Program Listing 10–1. "BREAKEVEN"

```
1000 REM PROGRAM "BREAKEVEN"
1020 PRINT "INPUT ALL COSTS IN DOLLARS"
1030 PRINT "WITH NO PUNCTUATION":PRINT
1040 INPUT "FIXED COST OF OPERATION";F
1050 INPUT "VARIABLE COSTS AS $$$  ";V
1060 INPUT "MAX POSSIBLE VOLUME $  ";M
1070 PRINT
1080 REM CALCULATE THE BREAK-EVEN POINT
1090 PRINT
1130 FOR X=1 TO 100
1140      S=X*(M/100)
1150      E=X*(V/100)+F
1160      IF E<S THEN 1180
1170 NEXT X
1180 LPRINT"FOR MAX SALES OF";M;"VARIABLE";V;"AND FIXED";F
1190 PRINT
1200 LPRINT USING "THE BREAK EVEN POINT IS   ##";S/100;
1210 LPRINT " PERCENT":LPRINT
1220 REM NOW FIND 5 PERCENT OF THE VALUES
1230 M1=M/20:V1=V/20:M2=M1:V2=V1
1240 REM
1250 LPRINT TAB(7);"SALES";TAB(19);"COSTS";TAB(30);"PROFIT";
1260 LPRINT TAB(40);"MARGIN"
1270 L$="    #######     #######     ######      ##"
1280 REM
1290 FOR X=1 TO 20
1300      P1=INT(M2-(V2+F)):P2=100*P1/M2:IF P2<2 THEN P2=0
1310      LPRINT USING L$;INT(M2);INT(V2)+F;P1;P2
1320      REM INCREMENT THE VALUES
1330      M2=M2+M1:V2=V2+V1
1340      REM
1350 NEXT X
1360 GOTO 1000
```

Now, consider the projected business activities for the next month. Based on the previous month's performance you may draw the graph in advance, making changes you believe will improve performance. This is also a simulation. If you can get a computer to do what you have just done by hand, you will have constructed a *computer model* of the events, and it will, hopefully, predict the future.

Simulation can be this simple or, given larger computers and people working full time on it, computer modeling can conceivably be used to predict the outcome of a war (this is done by the military forces as training) or to simulate some of the problems that will result from population growth or industrial expansion.

The first requirement in solving the break-even problem is to know, or to accurately estimate, the maximum possible volume of business that is possible under the present circumstances. A retail store's maximum might be based on the floor space where customers inspect the merchandise, the average size sale (from previous records), and the number of clerks available to ring up sales. There will be some upper limit; this is the "maximum sales" figure. The fixed operating costs must be known. These might include rent, lights, heat, advertising, and fixed salaries. Presumably, these "fixed costs" would be the same if nothing at all were to be sold. The remaining variable in the equation is the difference between cost and selling price; in other words, the markup. Say that goods cost 60% of retail and sales commissions are 10%; 70 cents of each sales dollar can be called "variable costs" because the cost varies in direct proportion to sales—with no sales there would be no variable costs.

We now have all the information necessary to calculate the profit for any volume of sales from zero to maximum. This technique is often associated with retail sales, but it is even more applicable to directly measurable tasks such as assembly-line production.

GRAPHICAL METHOD

Begin by drawing a graph similar to the one shown in Fig. 10-1, using scales that seem to be realistic for your business. The vertical scale represents zero at the bottom and maximum dollar volume at the top. The dashed line parallel to the bottom of the graph represents fixed costs. If you use a scale of $100,000 maximum and fixed costs are known to be $10,000, then the fixed-cost line will be 1/10th of the distance from the bottom line. Next, draw a sales line from the lower left corner to the upper right corner; any possible volume of sales now lies somewhere on this sloping line. Another sloping line represents variable costs. This will begin at zero as did the sales line—zero costs for zero sales. If your variable costs are 70%, then the variable-cost line must terminate at the 70% point on the vertical scale. Finally, draw another sloping line parallel to the variable-cost line, which represents the *total* of the fixed and variable costs. The graph is now complete.

The graph is interpreted as follows: The sloping line representing volume from zero to maximum, and the sloping line representing total costs (fixed + variable) will cross at some point. This is known as the *break-even point*. Sales above that point are profitable, while sales below that point result in a loss. Notice, also, that the margin of profit, or percentage of sales retained as earnings, rapidly becomes larger above the break-even point. Based on this simulation, the business may wish to change prices or other factors so as to make more profit or break even at a lower volume.

THE COMPUTER TECHNIQUE

As computer users our objective is to accomplish this same task by means of a program. The program will permit the viewing of several different scenarios by merely changing one or more of the key facts: fixed costs, variable costs (markup), full production, or the size of the facility.

Program Listing 10-1 is the program that may be used to accomplish what we just did by using a graph. This program is in the TRS-80 version of BASIC, and with minor modifications it can be used in most small machines. All the necessary data are input from the keyboard as the program runs, making this an exception to the general rule that business software must use disk files. An explanation of the program follows.

When the program opens, the operator is asked (lines 1040 to 1060) to input three figures: (1) the fixed costs, (2) the variable costs at full production, and (3) the maximum possible sales. These are dollar figures.

Next, the program calculates the break-even point. It does this by repeated comparison of the sales line with the total costs (that is, fixed plus variable) at each 1/10th of 1% of the vertical scale. This is done by the FOR-NEXT loop, lines 1130 through 1170. For example, at 10% of maximum (when X = 10) it adds the fixed costs to 10% of the variable cost and compares the total with sales.

When the program determines that costs have dropped below the sales figure for the first time, it leaves the loop and prints the value of X, which is the break-even point to within 1/10th of a percentage point. Line 1200 prints this value.

Line 1230 divides M and V into 5% increments as explained in the remark, line 1220. The loop, lines 1290 through 1350, calculates and prints, at these 5% increments, percent of maximum sales, actual sales, total cost of sales, profit, and margin in percent. The actual printout of a "run" of this program is shown in Fig. 10-2. The listing was made with fixed costs of $780, selling costs (variable) at 59.95% of retail, and the

FOR MAX SALES OF 10000 VARIABLE 5995 AND FIXED 780
THE BREAK EVEN POINT IS 19.5 PERCENT

SALES	COSTS	PROFIT	MARGIN
500	1079	-580	0
1000	1379	-380	0
1500	1679	-180	0
2000	1979	21	1
2500	2278	221	9
3000	2578	421	14
3500	2878	621	18
4000	3178	822	21
4500	3477	1022	23
5000	3777	1222	24
5500	4077	1422	26
6000	4377	1623	27
6500	4676	1823	28
7000	4976	2023	29
7500	5276	2223	30
8000	5576	2424	30
8500	5875	2624	31
9000	6175	2824	31
9500	6475	3024	32
10000	6775	3225	32

Fig. 10–2. Sample printout of the program, "BREAKEVEN."

total maximum sales of $10,000. By rerunning the program with different values, the store owner can immediately see the effect of the changes. Hopefully, he will not make any changes that are detrimental to his overall profit.

OTHER SIMULATION PROBLEMS

Many common business projections are a form of simulation. Cost analysis, for example, is a simulation if performed in advance of the actual events. A contractor making up a bid for a construction job is performing a simulation of that proposed activity. Calculations of past cost may be called models, and projections of future costs may be called simulations, but the terms are often used interchangeably. Very large construction companies routinely base their bid estimates on computer analysis.

One of the best uses of computer simulation involves the so-called "PERT" chart, or *critical path analysis* as it is sometimes called. This type of problem is best suited to the scheduling of a construction sequence or a production process. All of the identifiable main events are listed first, along with the time they are expected to take. If any event has to precede another, this is noted. For example, in building a house the foundation must precede the walls, and the walls precede the roof. This kind of program is not trivial and each one differs as the circumstances differ. The end purpose is to determine, in advance, possible "bottlenecks," as well as tasks that can be delayed if necessary. A "PERT" analysis might reveal that two tasks, neither dependent upon the other, can be performed simultaneously. One might have been scheduled to take four men six days, and the other to take two men ten days. Obviously, the labor may be rearranged so that both tasks are completed at the same time, allowing a task that follows both of the first two to be started sooner.

Fig. 10-3 demonstrates one way of schematically describing a critical path problem. This is an extremely simple example that can be solved by

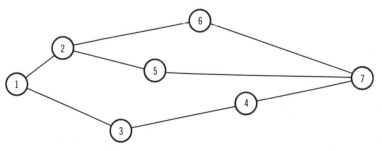

Fig. 10–3. A simple "PERT" chart.

inspection, which is the way contractors solved such problems for many years, before computer techniques were available to them. The *nodes*, or points where paths come together, are numbered 1 through 7; node 1 is the beginning of the diagram and node 7 is the final point, representing completion of the task. It is not necessary to have the paths represent any particular subtasks at this time; for illustration we simply assume that they do represent real events. We have further assumed that each subtask, or path between any two numbers, can be described as follows:

- Path 1 from node 1 to node 2; 2 increments of time.
- Path 2 from node 1 to node 3; 5 increments of time.
- Path 3 from node 3 to node 4; 3 increments of time.
- Path 4 from node 2 to node 5; 3 increments of time.
- Path 5 from node 2 to node 6; 5 increments of time.
- Path 6 from node 4 to node 7; 10 increments of time.
- Path 7 from node 5 to node 7; 4 increments of time.
- Path 8 from node 6 to node 7; 6 increments of time.

The "PERT" program, Program Listing 10-2, is presented as an example exercise and the reader should not assume that it will be

Program Listing 10-2. "PERT"

```
1000 DIM A(8,3)
1010 REM
1020 FOR X=1 TO 8
1030     FOR Y=0 TO 3
1040     READ A(X,Y)
1050     NEXT Y
1060 NEXT X
1070 DATA 1,1,2,2,2,1,3,5,3,3,4,3,4,2,5,3,5,2,6,5
1080 DATA 6,4,7,10,7,5,7,4,8,6,7,6
1090 LPRINT"PATH","FROM","TO","TIME"
1100 FOR X=1 TO 8
1110     FOR Y=0 TO 3
1120     LPRINT A(X,Y),
1130     NEXT Y
1140     LPRINT
1150 NEXT X
1160 LPRINT:LPRINT
1170 P=8:PS=A(8,2)
1180 LPRINT" FROM---TO--";TAB(42);"TIME"
1190 FOR X=P TO 1 STEP-1
1200     IF A(X,2)<P1 THEN 1300
1210     P1=A(X,1):P2=A(X,2):P3=A(X,3):P4=0
1220     P4=P4+P3:LPRINT P2;P1;
1230       FOR Y=X TO 1 STEP-1
1240       IF A(Y,2)<>P1 THEN 1270
1250       P1=A(Y,1):LPRINT A(Y,1);
1260       P4=P4+A(Y,3)
1270       NEXT Y
1280     LPRINT TAB(42);P4
1290 NEXT X
1300 PRINT "DONE"
```

sufficient for larger or more complex tasks. The fundamental techniques for analyzing multiple paths involve two major features: (1) storing the path descriptions in one or several arrays, and (2) providing a method of comparing them to find which paths are the most critical in terms of time. This demonstration program is in Microsoft BASIC, a version of which is available for most low-cost machines. If another dialect of BASIC is to be used, it may be necessary to use a different kind of PRINT statement. We first establish a three-dimensional array, A(8,3), and then read data into it with the nested loops, lines 1020–1060. (The data could have been as easily input from the keyboard, with an INPUT statement located within the loops.)

Fig. 10-4 is a schematic drawing of the array after the numbers have been read in. Remember that an array with a dimension of (8,3) actually contains nine rows and four columns.

Next, a set of nested loops, lines 1090–1150, reads the data out of the array and prints it in columns for the operator's inspection and approval. The printout lists the contents of the array, with headings to identify each column. This printing takes place at program lines 1090–1150. The first column of the printed information is the path number, the second and third columns are the "from" and "to" nodes that define that particular path, and the fourth column is the time needed for the subtask. It is now only necessary for the program to analyze the data and print its considered opinion of the overall job plan, as it has done in Fig. 10-5.

In the next and most important part of the operation, the program obtains the data by reading it from the arrays in the nested loops, lines 1190–1290. Notice that these are loops with a *negative index;* that is, they begin at their maximum value and are decremented by one on each iteration. Why? Only because we chose to read the data into the arrays in ascending order from the beginning to the end of the project, and, to analyze the paths, we want to start at completion time and work back to the beginning. The "X" loop reads the "to" nodes from the array starting with 7, the last node. The inner, or "Y" loop, reads the "from" nodes.

At line 1170 we have set a variable, P, equal to 8, the number of paths,

0,0	0,1	0,2	0,3	0,4	0,5	0,6	0,7	0,8
1,0	1,1	1,2	1,3	1,4	1,5	1,6	1,7	1,8
2,0	2,1	2,2	2,3	2,4	2,5	2,6	2,7	2,8
3,0	3,1	3,2	3,3	3,4	3,5	3,6	3,7	3,8

Fig. 10–4. A three-dimensional array.

PATH	FROM	TO	TIME
1	1	2	2
2	1	3	5
3	3	4	3
4	2	5	3
5	2	6	5
6	4	7	10
7	5	7	4
8	6	7	6

FROM---TO--				TIME
7	6	2	1	13
7	5	2	1	9
7	4	3	1	18
6	2	1		7
5	2	1		5
4	3	1		8
3	1			5
2	1			2

There are three complete paths between 7 and 1

Fig. 10–5. Sample printout of the program, "PERT."

and PS is set to the value of A(8,2). A(8,2) is the last (8th) value in the second column of the array; it is the terminal point or node for the overall project. The outer loop will read from P to 1, in steps of -1. This means that the loop index, X, will equal 8 when it begins, and 1 when it ends. Within the X loop, a test is made (line 1200) for the value of array segment, A(X,2). This quantity will represent the Xth value of the list of "from" numbers. In the first iteration of the X loop, X will be 8 and A(X,2) will be 6 (see printout, Fig. 10-5).

For each value of the X, or outer loop, the program tests A(X,2) to find a path it can follow. In the first iteration, using the numbers that have been read in for this example, a path is found to exist between nodes 7 and 6. Looking at the printout of the array in Fig. 10-5, it can be seen that this path (the one described as path 8) requires 6 increments of time to be completed. The time is accumulated in the variable, P4. The program continues a rather zig-zag course through the array, always looking for the next number toward the start. When it arrives at point 1, the beginning, it "knows" the several subpaths that have been taken, and the total time for those subpaths.

This activity continues with different values of X and Y until all complete paths, from end to beginning, have been explored. The lower part of the printout, Fig. 10-5, shows that the first path that was explored went from 7, to 6, to 2, to 1, with an accumulated time of 13 increments. A similar record of the other two complete paths is also printed. The program has now run its course for the values that were given to it.

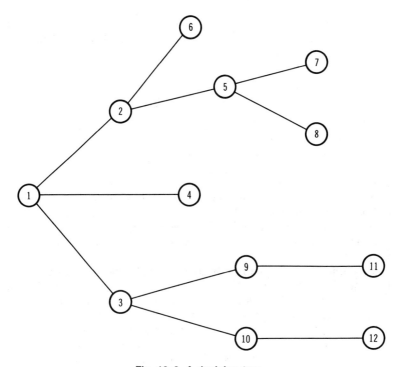

Fig. 10–6. A decision tree.

A more comprehensive and versatile critical path analysis, considerably more complex than this example, can be found in the book, "BASIC Programming," listed as a reference at the end of this chapter.[1] The example program we just examined will serve as an introduction to this most interesting subject.

The aforementioned book, by Drs. Kemeny and Kurtz, also contains a section on the use of "decision-tree" programs. These types of programs contain, as data, a number of different courses of action and the probable results of those actions. A program begins at a fixed point and then branches to several different possible paths. Each of those paths has several possible outcomes. The purpose of such a program is to check each combination of paths and find the one that is most profitable, or that otherwise meets some desired criteria. Buying and selling shares on the stock market is one such use and, in fact, is illustrated in the book.

A sample decision tree can be seen by inspecting Fig. 10-6. The decision tree somewhat resembles the PERT chart, with one very important difference. The PERT concept requires that all paths come together at the completion of the project. The decision tree continues to branch until it has chosen *one out of many* possible end points. It should be noted that the decision tree is the basis for many computer chess and checkers programs, as well as for other kinds of simulation. The principle is that completion of any possible move results in several new choices being offered.

RANDOM NUMBERS

It has been suggested that games are examples of real-life simulations. High-quality games and simulations represent a very complex kind of programming. Games make wide use of random numbers to simulate chance. Most computer languages of any note contain, as a built-in function, a random-number generator, which can be called into action by the statement RND(0), or some similar statement. In some versions of BASIC, the numbers are limited to the range of 0 to 1, and must be multiplied by 100, for example, if you need random numbers between 0 and 100. Other versions of BASIC provide a wider range of random numbers.

This function permits the introduction of chance into an otherwise fixed sequence of events. For example, a deck of cards contains 52 discrete cards, but the order in which they are presented to the players, following the shuffle, is mostly a matter of random selection. It is extremely easy to incorporate this feature into programs. In programs involving the simulation of a card game, five cards may be "dealt" by generating five random numbers between 1 and 52, representing five cards. Of course, a record must be kept to prevent the same card from being "dealt" more than once.

Program Listing 10-3 is a small program segment that generates

Program Listing 10–3. "RANDOMIZE"

```
1000 REM PROGRAM "RANDOMIZE"
1010 FOR X=1 TO 5
1020     PRINT INT(52*(RND(-1)));
1030 NEXT X


RUN

 8 51 37 22 35
RUN

 14 44 22 44 15
RUN

 32 7 39 1 15
RUN

 4 23 28 32 49
```

random numbers in the range of 0 to 52. Four sample runs are listed following the program lines. As can be seen, there are a few duplications among the numbers printed by the program. Fig. 10-7 demonstrates one possible way to avoid "dealing" the same number twice. In this illustration, two segments of an array are established; one segment holds consecutive numbers which correspond to possible random numbers that may be generated, and the other side-by-side segment is initialized to contain zeros. Each time a number in the random-number row has been chosen by the program, a 1 is written into the matching array cell to indicate that that random number has been "used." Thus, the random numbers are "checked off" as they are used, to prevent any from being used more than once. The program will have a means of looking through the list to see if a given number has been used. If it has, the program will keep generating numbers until it finds an unused one. In this manner each number will be "dealt" only one time in each game or simulation, and the possibility of having six or eight "aces" on the table at one time will be completely avoided.

The references at the end of this chapter also include a book on how computer games are written and one on the subject of simulations. The latter touches on such fields as simulation of motion and simulation of electronic circuit performance. The reader who is past the point of more common varieties of programming is encouraged to research these subjects. A good workout on the use of arrays is guaranteed. As simulation is one of the most complex and creative areas for computer programming and no one general technique can be described here in enough detail to be useful, the reader is encouraged to research the subject with regard to his or her own business specialty. As more and more small computers are becoming available with good graphics capability, it should be possible for many computer owners to graphically illustrate their simulations on the video terminal and, in some cases, on the printer.

Given their power to quickly analyze great quantities of data, it was perhaps inevitable that computers would sooner or later be used in real-life decision making. At the time this book is being written, most large businesses are routinely using computers for accounting and inventory purposes and they are beginning to trust executive planning and decisions to their computers. As in other fields, the results can be no

1	2	3	4	5	6	7	8	9	10	11	12	13	14	15	16	RANDOM NUMBER
0	0	1	1	0	1	0	0	0	0	1	0	0	1	1	1	"CHECK OFF"

Fig. 10–7. Using an array to "check off" random-number selection.

better and no worse than the data input and the quality of the programming. Managers with little or no understanding of computers are certain to be pushed aside by those who can control and use the power of these machines. Rather than being slaves of these machines, those who look to the future will be their masters.

SELF-HELP TEST QUESTIONS

1. What is a computer simulation?
2. What is the "break-even" point for a business?
3. Name three other types of modeling or simulation.
4. How do computers simulate the laws of chance?
5. What limits the accuracy of a computer simulation?

REFERENCES

1. Kemeny, J. G.; Kurtz, T. E. *BASIC Programming*, 2nd ed. John Wiley & Sons, Inc., New York, 1971.

2. Liffick, B.; *et al. Simulation.* Byte Publications, Inc., Peterborough, NH.

3. Spencer, D. D. *Game Playing With Computers*, 2nd ed. Hayden Book Co., Inc., Rochelle Park, NJ, 1975.

ASCII Code Chart

LEAST SIGNIFICANT BITS

<table>
<tr><td></td><td></td><td>000</td><td>001</td><td>010</td><td>011</td><td>100</td><td>101</td><td>110</td><td>111</td><td></td></tr>
<tr><td></td><td>00000</td><td>NUL</td><td>SOH</td><td>STX</td><td>ETX</td><td>EOT</td><td>ENQ</td><td>ACK</td><td>BEL</td><td>CONTROL</td></tr>
<tr><td></td><td>00001</td><td>BS</td><td>HT</td><td>LF</td><td>VT</td><td>FF</td><td>CR</td><td>SO</td><td>SI</td><td>FUNC-</td></tr>
<tr><td></td><td>00010</td><td>DLE</td><td>DCI</td><td>DC2</td><td>DC3</td><td>DC4</td><td>NAK</td><td>SYN</td><td>ETB</td><td>TIONS</td></tr>
<tr><td></td><td>00011</td><td>CAN</td><td>EM</td><td>SUB</td><td>ESC</td><td>FS</td><td>GS</td><td>RS</td><td>US</td><td></td></tr>
<tr><td></td><td>00100</td><td>SP</td><td>!</td><td>"</td><td>#</td><td>$</td><td>%</td><td>&</td><td>"</td><td></td></tr>
<tr><td></td><td>00101</td><td>(</td><td>)</td><td>*</td><td>+</td><td>,</td><td>−</td><td>.</td><td>/</td><td></td></tr>
<tr><td>MOST</td><td>00110</td><td>0</td><td>1</td><td>2</td><td>3</td><td>4</td><td>5</td><td>6</td><td>7</td><td></td></tr>
<tr><td>SIGNIF-</td><td>00111</td><td>8</td><td>9</td><td>:</td><td>;</td><td><</td><td>=</td><td>></td><td>?</td><td></td></tr>
<tr><td>ICANT</td><td>01000</td><td>@</td><td>A</td><td>B</td><td>C</td><td>D</td><td>E</td><td>F</td><td>G</td><td></td></tr>
<tr><td>BITS</td><td>01001</td><td>H</td><td>I</td><td>J</td><td>K</td><td>L</td><td>M</td><td>N</td><td>O</td><td></td></tr>
<tr><td></td><td>01010</td><td>P</td><td>Q</td><td>R</td><td>S</td><td>T</td><td>U</td><td>V</td><td>W</td><td></td></tr>
<tr><td></td><td>01011</td><td>X</td><td>Y</td><td>Z</td><td>[</td><td>\</td><td>]</td><td>↑</td><td>—</td><td></td></tr>
<tr><td></td><td>01100</td><td>'</td><td>a</td><td>b</td><td>c</td><td>d</td><td>e</td><td>f</td><td>g</td><td></td></tr>
<tr><td></td><td>01101</td><td>h</td><td>i</td><td>j</td><td>k</td><td>l</td><td>m</td><td>n</td><td>o</td><td></td></tr>
<tr><td></td><td>01110</td><td>p</td><td>q</td><td>r</td><td>s</td><td>t</td><td>u</td><td>v</td><td>w</td><td></td></tr>
<tr><td></td><td>01111</td><td>x</td><td>y</td><td>z</td><td>{</td><td>:</td><td>}</td><td>∿</td><td>DEL</td><td></td></tr>
</table>

Control Character Functions

NUL = Null
SOH = Start of Heading
STX = Start of Text
ETX = End of Text
EOT = End of Transmission
ENQ = Enquiry
ACK = Acknowledge
BEL = Bell (ring)
BS = Backspace
HT = Horizontal Tabulation
LF = Line Feed
VT = Vertical Tabulation
FF = Form Feed
CR = Carriage Return
SO = Shift Out
SI = Shift In

DLE = Data Link Escape
DC1 = Device Control 1
DC2 = Device Control 2
DC3 = Device Control 3
DC4 = Device Control 4 (Stop)
NAK = Negative Acknowledge
SYN = Synchronous Idle
ETB = End of Transmission Block
CAN = Cancel
EM = End of Medium
SUB = Substitute
ESC = Escape
FS = File Separator
GS = Group Separator
RS = Record Separator
US = Unit Separator
DEL = Delete

Glossary

BASIC—Acronym for *Beginner's All-purpose Symbolic Instruction Code.* A high-level computer language in which most business programs are written. (Others are RPG, FORTRAN, COBOL, etc.)

Byte—A unit of data storage roughly equivalent to one alphabetic or numeric character. (Diskette or memory storage space is usually measured in bytes.)

Diskette—A flexible record-like magnetic disk on which data and programs are stored. The disk is permanently encased in a square paper or plastic jacket.

Disk Operating System (DOS)—See **Operating System.**

Documentation—Instruction or operation manuals for hardware or software.

Floppy-Disk Drive—A mechanism into which a diskette is inserted in order to read data from it or write data on it.

Hard Copy—Data output on paper from a printer.

Hardware—Computer, printer, terminal, and other equipment.

K—Abbreviation for 1024. For example, 32K of memory means a storage capacity of 32,768 bytes.

Memory—The part of the computer that stores programs and data.

Microcomputer—Typical single-user computer.

Minicomputer—A multiuser computer, able to process larger amounts of data at one time.

Modem—Acoustic coupling device that allows data to be transmitted and received over telephone lines.

Operating System—Program consisting of a group of utility programs that handle communications between the computer and its peripherals.

Peripherals—Extra add-on hardware, such as terminals, disk drives, modems, and printers.

Software—The programmed instructions that tell the computer what to do.

Time Sharing—The use of one computer by more than one user at a time.

Word Processing—Electronic typing and editing.

Index

READER SERVICE CARD

To better serve you, the reader, please take a moment to fill out this card, or a copy of it, for us. Not only will you be kept up to date on the Blacksburg Series books, but as an extra bonus, **we will randomly select five cards every month, from all of the cards sent to us during the previous month. The names that are drawn will win, absolutely free, a book from the Blacksburg Continuing Education Series.** Therefore, make sure to indicate your choice in the space provided below. For a complete listing of all the books to choose from, refer to the inside front cover of this book. Please, one card per person. Give everyone a chance.

In order to find out who has won a book in your area, call (703) 953-1861 anytime during the night or weekend. When you do call, an answering machine will let you know the monthly winners. Too good to be true? Just give us a call. Good luck.

If I win, please send me a copy of:

_____

I understand that this book will be sent to me absolutely free, if my card is selected.

For our information, how about telling us a little about yourself. We are interested in your occupation, how and where you normally purchase books and the books that you would like to see in the Blacksburg Series. We are also interested in finding authors for the series, so if you have a book idea, write to The Blacksburg Group, Inc., P.O. Box 242, Blacksburg, VA 24060 and ask for an Author Packet. We are also interested in TRS-80, APPLE, OSI and PET BASIC programs.

My occupation is _____

I buy books through/from _____

Would you buy books through the mail? _____

I'd like to see a book about _____

Name _____

Address _____

City _____

State _____ Zip _____

MAIL TO: BOOKS, BOX 715, BLACKSBURG, VA 24060
!!!!!PLEASE PRINT!!!!!